6

Skills

Problem Solving and Reasoning

Karen Morrison
Lisa Greenstein

OXFORD

Great Clarendon Street, Oxford, OX2 6DP, United Kingdom

Oxford University Press is a department of the University of Oxford. It furthers the University's objective of excellence in research, scholarship, and education by publishing worldwide. Oxford is a registered trade mark of Oxford University Press in the UK and in certain other countries.

First published in 2024

British Library Cataloguing in Publication Data
Data available

9781382044561

10 9 8 7 6 5 4 3 2 1

Paper used in the production of this book is a natural, recyclable product made from wood grown in sustainable forests.

The manufacturing process conforms to the environmental regulations of the country of origin.

Printed in China by Golden Cup

Acknowledgements
The publisher and authors would like to thank the following for permission to use photographs and other copyright material:

Photos: p8(t): A1.VIEWS / Shutterstock; **p8(b)**: Napat / Shutterstock; **p15(t):** MediaNews Group / Orange County Register via Getty Images; **p16(l)**: Globe Turner / Shutterstock; **p16(m)**: Oxford Fajar / crystal; **p16(r)**: Alexander Yurkevich / Shutterstock; **p18**: Sklep Spozywczy / Shutterstock; **p19**: S.Borisov / Shutterstock; **p20:** VectorMine / Shutterstock; **p33:** Jirayu wannagul / Shutterstock; **p34:** Ilona Ignatova / Shutterstock; **p36:** supakrit tirayasupasin / Shutterstock; **p37:** Bruno Schmidiger / Panther Media GmbH / Alamy Stock Photo; **p42:** svo2302 / Shutterstock; **p49:** Nostalgia for Infinity / Shutterstock; **p52:** MNStudio / Shutterstock; **p53:** Hero Images / Getty Images; p54: ixpert / Shutterstock; **p55:** Mdesignstudio / Shutterstock; **p56:** Rudra Narayan Mitra / Shutterstock; **p58(t):** Robyn Mackenzie / Shutterstock; **p58(m), p59(b)**: 123RF; **p58(bl)**: Sergej Razvodovskij / Shutterstock; **p58(br)**: akepong srichaichana / Shutterstock; **p59(t)**: Jiri Hera / Shutterstock; **p60:** Mathew Risley / Shutterstock; **p61:** Leena Azzam / Shutterstock; **p62:** soft_light / Shutterstock; **p63:** Sharon Morris / Shutterstock; **p64:** NAMGYAL SHERPA / Stringer / Getty Images; **p65(t)**: Morozov67 / Shutterstock; **p65(b)**: Daniel Prudek / Shutterstock; **p66:** Slawomir Fajer / Shutterstock; **p68:** NOVODIASTOCK / Shutterstock; **p70, 71**: Margaret M Stewart / Shutterstock; **p74(t)**: svry / Shutterstock; **p74(bl)**: JIANG HONGYAN / Shutterstock; **p74(br)**: Shaiith / Shutterstock; **p75:** ytyoung / Shutterstock; **p77(l)**: Ivonne Wierink / Shutterstock; **p77(r)**: Roman Sigaev / Shutterstock; **p77(b)**: Igor Dutina / Shutterstock.

Cover art: Andrea Manzati

Artwork by: Katya Balakina, Q2A Media and Oxford University Press.

Every effort has been made to contact copyright holders of material reproduced in this book. Any omissions will be rectified in subsequent printings if notice is given to the publisher.

Contents

My problem-solving record

These are the steps I follow to solve a problem…

1 Read and understand the problem → 2 Choose a strategy

These are the strategies I tried…

Model the problem
- use objects
- draw bar models

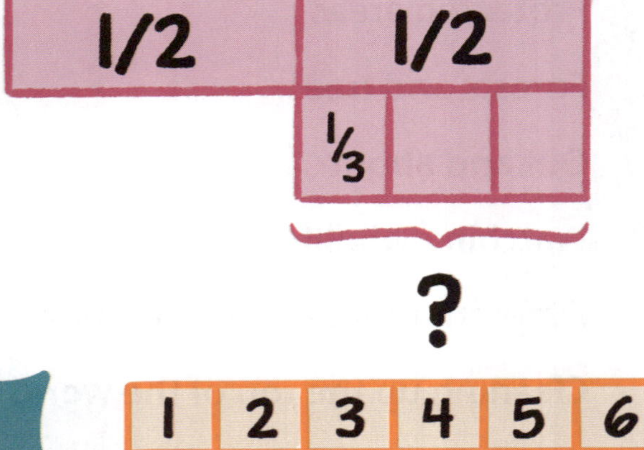

Guess, check and improve

2 X 4 = 8 Too small

2 X 6 = 12 Too big

2 X 5 = 10 ✓

1 2 3 4 5 6

Draw diagrams or graphs

2 KM ← → 5 KM

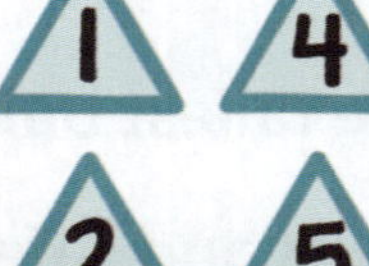

4 Check my answers

Use a table or an organized list

red + yellow

red + blue

yellow + blue

1	4
2	5
3	6

Write a number sentence

10 − ? = 3

1	2	3	4	5	6

1 Small businesses

Think, talk, reason

1 Laila's community is holding a fair to raise money for local charities.

a Where is the fair going to be held? ____________________

b When will it take place? ____________________

c How long will it be on for? ____________________

2 The organizers of the fair charge an entry fee. The fee includes a snack and a cold drink. They decide to charge £3 for children and double that for adults.

a Sal paid £9 on entry fees. What is the most and least number of people Sal could have paid for?

____

b The Meyer family paid £21 for entry fees. How many adults and how many children could there be?

____

There are several possible answers. Each option must have at least one adult and at least one child.

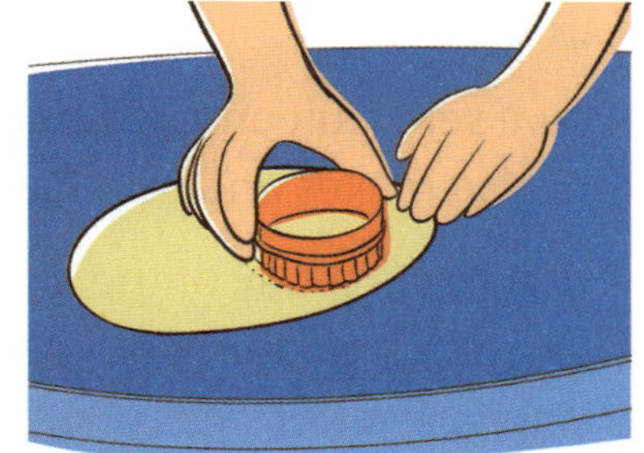

3 Laila decides to bake biscuits for the fete. She has a rectangular baking tray that is 36 cm wide and 46 cm long. The recipe says that she must place the biscuits at least 2 cm apart from each other, and at least 1 cm away from the edge of the baking tray.

Laila's biscuit cutter makes round biscuits with an 8 cm diameter.

What is the greatest number of biscuits she can fit on the baking tray?

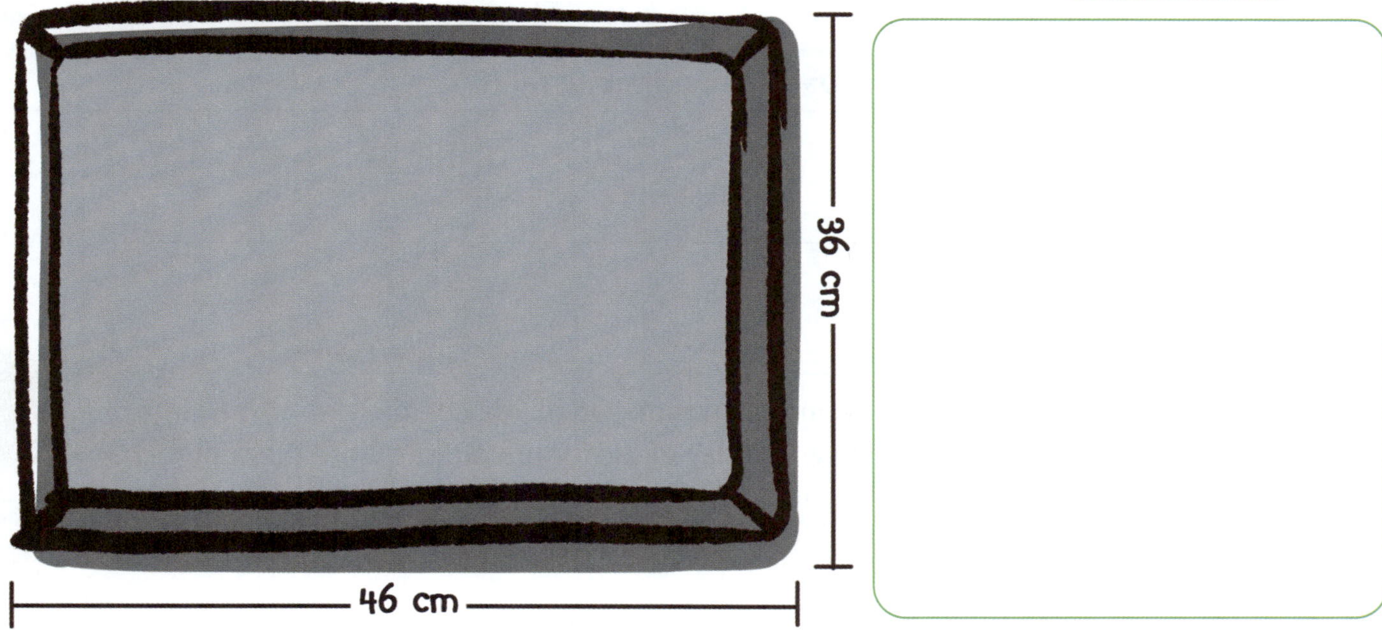

4 Laila sells biscuits for 50p each. She also sells ice lollies that cost 25p each. Zane has £3.00 to spend. Zane spends all his money and he buys both biscuits and ice lollies. How many of each could he buy?

Let's solve …

Aviwe sells fruit and vegetables at the local market. She also makes and sells fresh juices.

1 On the first day of the month, Aviwe sold 5 pomegranates. Each day after that, she increased her sales of pomegranates by three. She keeps track of sales in a table.

Daily pomegranate sales											
Day	1										
Sales	5										

Aviwe closed her stall for two days during the month. On the day before she closed, she sold 29 pomegranates. On which day of the month did she close the stall?

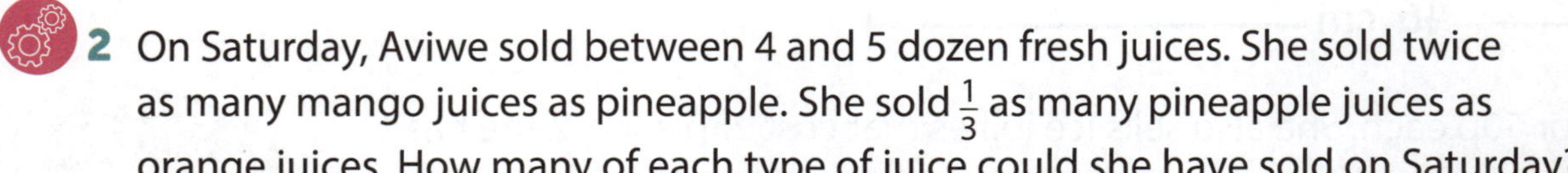

2 On Saturday, Aviwe sold between 4 and 5 dozen fresh juices. She sold twice as many mango juices as pineapple. She sold $\frac{1}{3}$ as many pineapple juices as orange juices. How many of each type of juice could she have sold on Saturday?

3 Aviwe has several 20p and 50p coins in her cashbox. Together, the coins total £9.90. If she has 27 coins altogether, how many of each coin could she have?

4 On Sunday, Aviwe had 240 ripe mangoes on the stall. She sold $\frac{3}{4}$ of them. On the way home, she gave $\frac{1}{3}$ of the leftover mangoes to her neighbours. How many did she have left?

a Add labels to this bar model to represent the problem.

not sold ___ of 240

b Work out the solution.

5 Ms Mati paid £3.10 for seven peaches and four oranges. Mr Smit paid £2.95 for four peaches and seven oranges. They want to work out the cost of one peach.

a In your group, discuss strategies they could use to do this.

b Choose the strategy you like best. Use it to solve the problem.

Think, talk, reason

As a project, Stage 6 students work in groups to start and run their own small businesses. Each student will get an equal share of the money they make to donate to a charity of their choice.

1 Work in pairs. Read the information about four businesses and how much money they made in the first month. Then discuss these questions.

- **a** What makes a business successful?
- **b** Which of these businesses do you think was the most successful? Why?

Clean Sweep Yard Clearing

Nic and Emma made £26

Car Cleaners Inc

Laura, Zaf and Mai made £42

Crafty Cards

Kino, Li, Cara and Rob made £52

We Recycle 4U

Sal, Kai, Molly, Jo and Mario made £60

2 A local business offers to double the money that each business makes.

Write numbers to complete these sentences.

- **a** For every £1 the students make, they will get another £ ______________ from the local business.
- **b** Car Cleaners Inc will have £ ______________ once their money is doubled.
- **c** Once their money is doubled, each member of Crafty Cards will have £ ______________ to donate to charity.

3 Nic tells Emma that it is better to split the money equally between them before it is doubled. Emma says it makes no difference. Who is correct? Why?

4 We Recycle 4U collected 48 kilograms of recycling in two containers. One container was three times heavier than the other. How many kilograms of recycling were in each container?

5 As the project goes on, more local businesses get involved. In the second month, a local store sponsors two businesses. They agree to triple the money that the students make.

a Bike Delivery is a business set up by 8 students. They make £64.
How much will the store pay for each £1 they made?

b What will each student's share of the tripled money be?

c We Shop 4U is a business set up by 10 students. They make £93.50.
How much will the store pay to triple that amount?

d How much money will each student be able to donate to charity?

Think, talk, solve

The Stage 6 class are doing a project. Each group collects data about a small local business. Naresh's parents have a car wash business, so his group collected data there.

The car wash offers 4 different services:

Window cleaning £3

Quick wash and vacuum £5

Wash, vacuum and clean wheels £7

Wash, vacuum, clean wheels and polish £10

1 Naresh kept a tally of the services that people used in one day.

Services	Morning session	Afternoon session
Window cleaning	𝍸 𝍸 𝍸 𝍸 |	𝍸 𝍸 ||||
Quick wash and vacuum	𝍸 𝍸 𝍸 |	𝍸 𝍸 𝍸 |||
Wash, vacuum and clean wheels	𝍸 𝍸 |	𝍸 𝍸 𝍸 ||
Wash, vacuum, clean wheels and polish	𝍸	𝍸 ||

a Which service is most popular? ____________________________

b Was the car wash busier in the morning or the afternoon? Give a reason for your answer.

c How many cars did the car wash clean altogether?

Tell your partner what strategy you used to work this out.

2 Naresh and his group want to work out how much money the business made from 'Quick wash and vacuum' services made in the morning session.

This is how Asuka, Maria and Juan start to think about the problem:

Asuka

Maria

Juan

a Work with a partner to complete each person's strategy.

b How would you have worked this out? Why?

3 How can you work out how much money the car wash received on that day using the fewest calculations?

Share your ideas in your group.

Work out the solution using as few calculations as you can.

Think, talk, solve

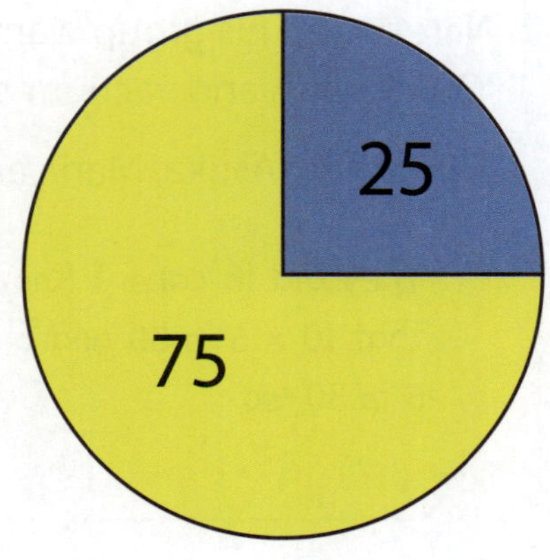

Shark Tank is a TV show. People with a good business idea can go on the show and try to convince **investors** to give them money to develop their ideas. The investors get a share of the business so that they get a share of the money the business makes when it is successful. For example, they might ask for a 25% share of ownership.

1 Sofi Overton (13) went on Shark Tank with her Wise Pockets Products – leggings and socks with pockets on them for phones and other devices.

a Discuss these questions in your group.

- Where do you think Sofi got the idea for her products?
- What sort of questions do you think the investors might ask her?
- Would you invest in this business? Give reasons for your decisions.

b One of the investors offered to give Sofi $30 000 and take a 33.3% share in the business. Sofi convinced them to give her $35 000 for a 25% share. Complete these sentences.

- Sofi got $ ______________ more than she was first offered.
- The investor got ______________% less of the business than they first offered.
- The business was valued at $140 000. This means that a 25% share was worth

  $______________.

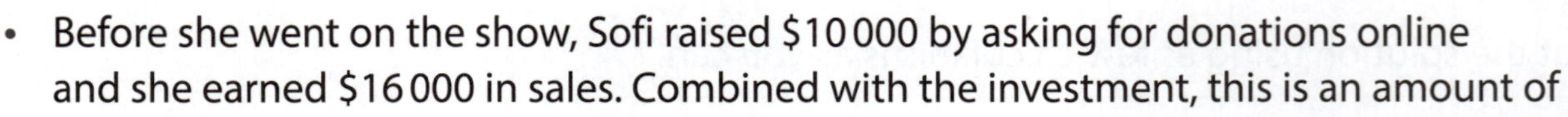

- Before she went on the show, Sofi raised $10 000 by asking for donations online and she earned $16 000 in sales. Combined with the investment, this is an amount of

  $______________.

2 At the time of the show, the socks sold for $15 a pair or $42 for a 3-pack.

a How much do you save per pair by buying the 3-pack?

____

b What would the company earn if they sold 94 pairs of socks and 108 3-packs?

____

____

3 Carson Kropfl (12) invented the Locker Board. This is a small skateboard that can fit into a backpack or school locker.

a Carson's company was valued at $325 000 at the time of the show.
An investor gave him $65 000 and asked for a 20% share of the company. What is 20% of the company's value?

____

b Since the show, the value of the company increased by 3000%. Use a calculator to work out the new value. Write a number sentence to show what you worked out:

____

4 An advert for the skateboard gives this information:

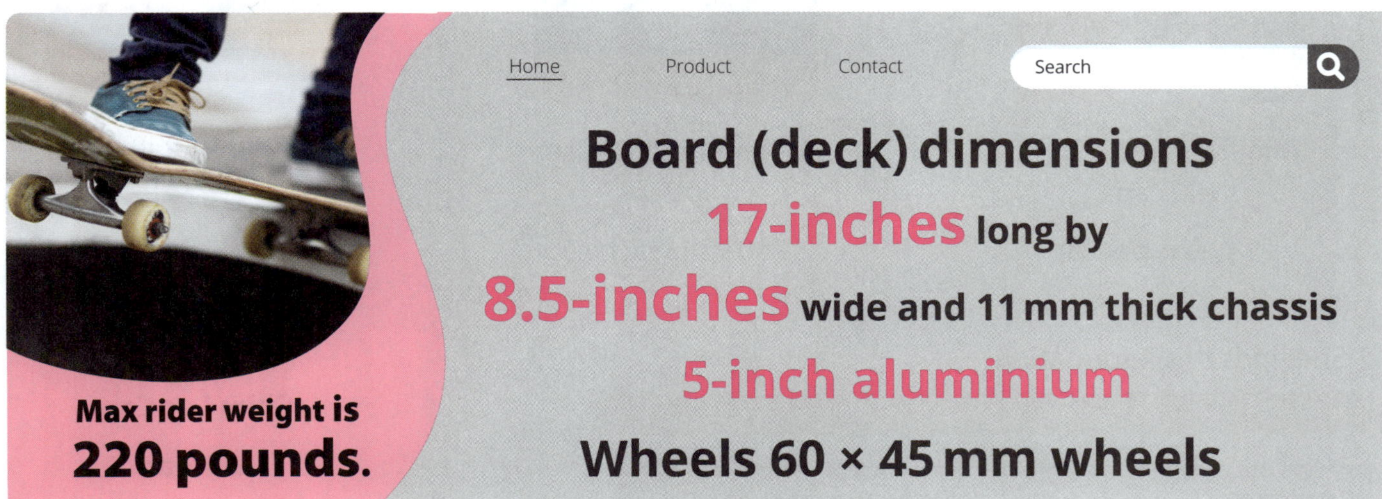

a Circle all the metric measurements.

b Is the board suitable for a 102 kg adult? ______________

c Write the dimensions of the skateboard deck in cm on this diagram.

Use a calculator to work out its volume in centimetres cubed (cm^3).

One pound is approximately 0.45 kg.

One inch is equivalent to 2.54 cm.

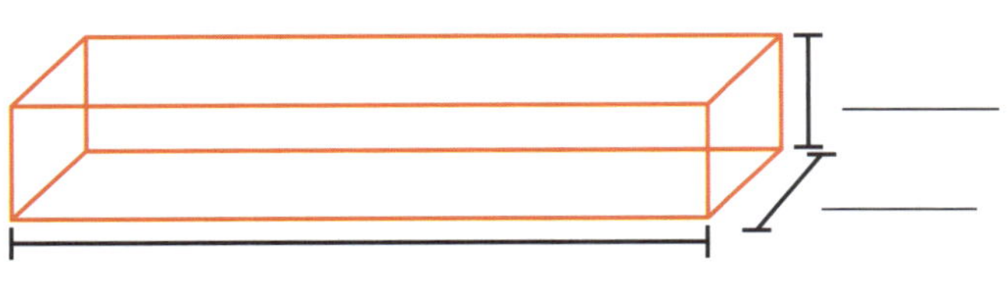

Think, talk, reason

Suki buys **imported** caps from a local wholesaler. She embroiders flowers onto them and sells them at the market.

1 Suki decides to find out how much it will cost her to import the caps herself.

La Gorra Caps

Mexico

Minimum purchase:
100 caps

21 pesos per cap

Dok Champa Caps

Laos

Minimum purchase:
100 caps

35 000 kip each cap

Terrific Tiger Caps

Malaysia

Minimum purchase:
100 caps

9 ringgits per cap

Chim Lac Caps

Vietnam

Minimum purchase:
100 caps

28 550 dong each cap

She finds this information.

Currency	Exchange rate for £1
Mexican peso	21.89
Lao kip	22 119.75
Malaysian ringgit	5.73
Vietnamese dong	29 130.50

The exchange rate table tells you how much of the other money has the same value as one British pound.

a Work out the price per cap in pounds to see which is the cheapest country to import them from.

b Compare your method of working with a partner.

2 Suki also investigates the cost of shipping and importing the caps.

Shipping costs (£) per carton (100 caps)

Mexico £108
Malaysia £32
Laos £56
Vietnam £52

Taxes and duties

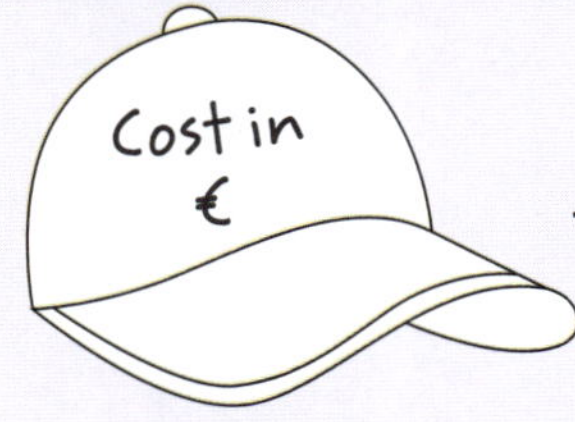

+

+

Work out the price including shipping, VAT and import duty of a cap from each country.

Turn back to page 4 and complete the problem-solving record.

2 Green spaces

Think, talk, write

Urban parks are green spaces in cities. There are many important reasons that people create parks in cities. They are places where people can relax and exercise. The plants produce oxygen, purifying the air and keeping the city cool. Parks also provide a place for birds, insects and other wildlife.

1 Read the information above about parks. Identify one reason that belongs in each column. Work with a partner to find more reasons to add to each column of the table.

Benefits of parks in cities

For people	For animals	For the environment

Let's solve ...

2 This table gives you information about the fraction of land made up of public green space (such as parks and public gardens) in some places around the world. Complete the table so that the information is presented in three different ways – as a fraction, as a percentage and as a decimal.

Place	What proportion of land in the city is public green space?		
	Percentage	**Fraction**	**Decimal**
Vienna, Austria	50%		
New York, USA		$\frac{27}{100}$	
Paris, France			0.1
Sydney, Australia		$\frac{23}{50}$	
Edinburgh, Scotland			0.49
Oslo, Norway		$\frac{17}{25}$	
Amsterdam, Netherlands	13%		

3 Which of the cities listed in the table has the greatest proportion of public green space?

____

4 Explain what you understand by the word proportion.

5 Use the information in the table to complete these statements.

a In Vienna, for every 5 km^2 of built urban environment, there is ____________ km^2 of green space.

b In Oslo, for every 500 km^2 of built urban environment, there is ____________ km^2 of green space.

6 Choose one of the other cities to make your own calculation.

In ______________________________, for every

____________ km^2 of built urban environment, there is

____________ km^2 of green space.

The built environment refers to city space roads, buildings or other structures that are not green space.

Let's reason …

1 Discuss with a partner. How could you sort these leaf shapes into five main categories? What are the main similarities and differences in the shapes?

Botanists classify leaves according to their shape. This poster shows you some common leaf shapes.

2 Henry explores the angles that he finds in the leaves. He draws a straight line through the stem. Then he constructs an angle where the leaf meets the stem.

Measure each angle using a protractor.

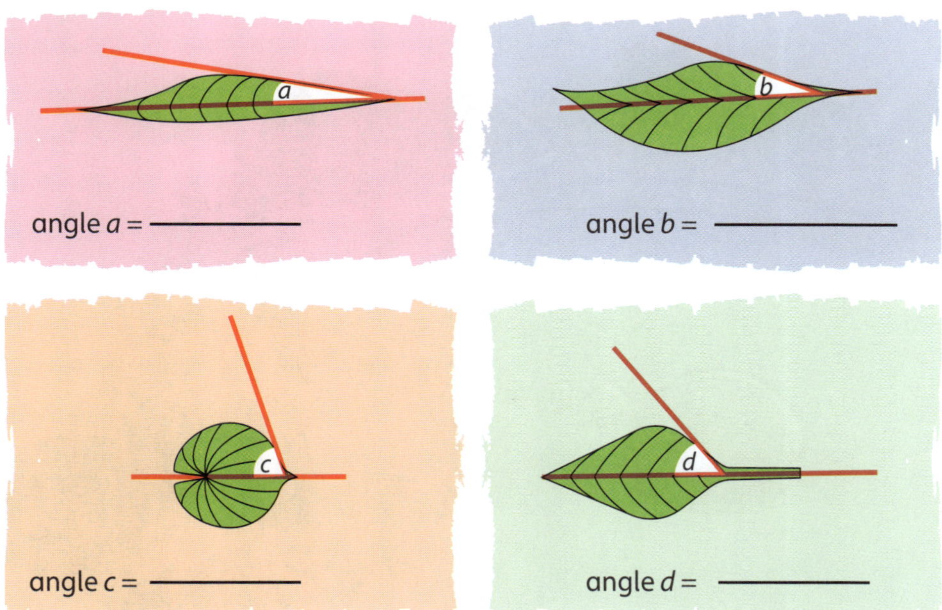

3 Use Henry's method for constructing angles. Choose six of the leaves from the poster. Draw over the pictures on page 20. Use a ruler to construct the angle to show how the leaf meets the stem. Measure the angle using a protractor. Complete the table to show which leaves you choose, and the size of each angle.

Name of leaf shape	Size of angle

4 Draw leaf shapes that match these polygons:

a right-angled triangle

b pentagon

c quadrilaterals with two angles bigger than 90° and two angles smaller than 90°.

The designers of a park decide to create a pond. Around the outside of the pond there will be rocks and plants, and, in the middle, there will be a platform where people can pose for pictures. There will also be a path of stepping stones to reach the platform.

1 For each question about the design, explain which part of the circle it deals with. Use one of the terms from the box. Write or draw a diagram to show what you mean.

centre diameter radius circumference

a How many rocks are needed around the edge?

b How long is the path of stepping stones?

c Where should the platform go?

d If the stepping stones go from one edge of the pond to the platform and straight across to the other side, how many are needed?

2 Kayley's park has a pond designed to look like a compass. It has four markers placed in the positions of north, south, east and west.

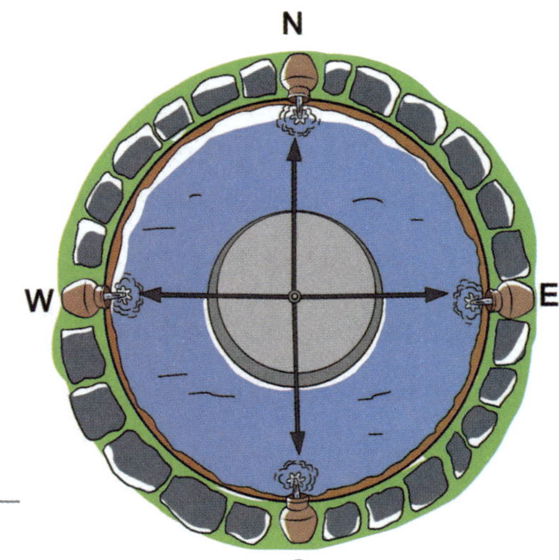

a Kayley walks from the south marker to the west marker. Her fitness tracker shows that she walked 3.2 metres. How can she use this distance to calculate the circumference?

____

b A real compass sometimes has additional markers at northeast (NE), southeast (SE), southwest (SW) and northwest (NW). If the pond had these, what would be the distance from each marker to the next?

____

3 Before the sun rises, the pond is in the shade. Later in the day, less of the pond is in the shade and more is in the sun. At 9 a.m., $\frac{3}{4}$ of the pond is in the shade. By 10 a.m. another fifth of the pond is in the sun.

a What fraction of the pond is in the sun by 10 a.m.? ______________________________

b Express this as a percentage. ______________________________

c How much of the pond would you estimate was in the sun by 9:30 a.m.? Explain to a partner how you worked it out.

Think, talk, reason

Some parks have special facilities where you can have a picnic. The designers of this park created their picnic area like this.

- Each picnic table has 2 benches.
- Three people can fit on a bench.
- There is one cooking zone for every 2 picnic tables.
- There is one washing area for every cooking zone.

1 Complete the table.

Number of picnic tables	2	4	6	8	10	12	14	16	18	20
Number of benches	4	8								
Number of people who can be seated at tables (seating places)	12	24								
Number of cooking zones	1	2								
Number of washing areas	1									

Let's solve ...

2 A **ratio** tells you how much of one item or quantity there is compared with another. Read how these students explain their understanding of ratios.

Using what you understand from these students, work out the missing amounts:

a If there are 25 picnic tables, there must be ____________ benches.

b If there are 280 benches, there must be ____________ picnic tables.

Explain to a partner the maths you used to work these out.

3 Write the following as ratios.

a seating places : benches ____________

b picnic table : cooking zones ____________

c cooking zones : seating places ____________

4 Use the ratios to complete the following statements. Use your own choice of 3-digit or 4-digit numbers.

a If there are ____________ benches, there are ____________ seating places.

b If there are ____________ picnic tables, there are ____________ benches.

c If there are ____________ cooking zones, there are ____________ seating places.

The management of an urban park decided to survey some of the visitors to the park. Look at their **findings** and answer the questions.

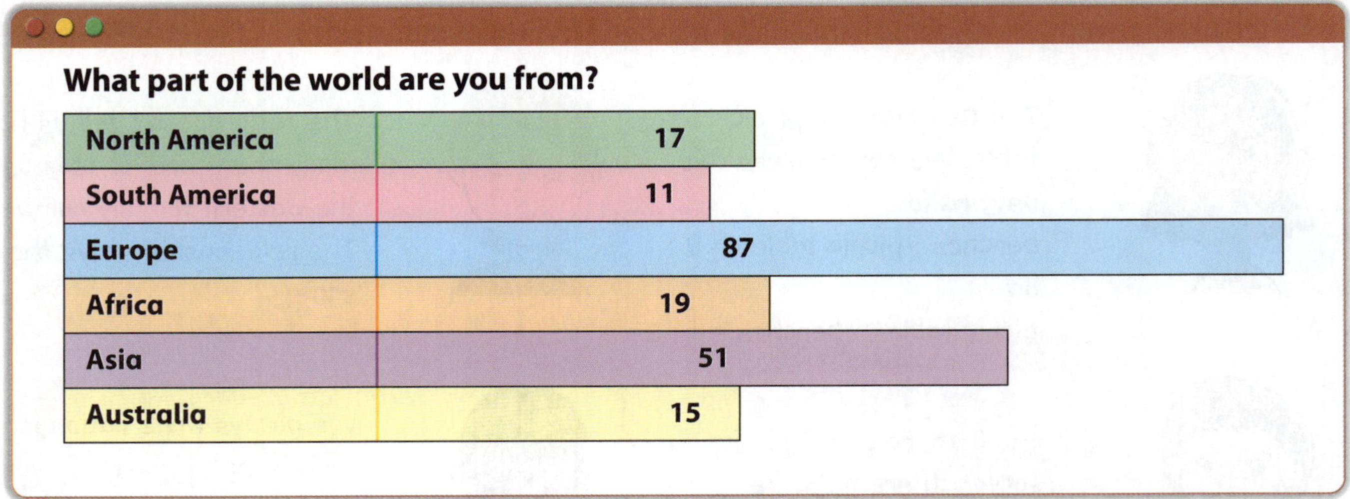

1 **a** How many people did the researchers ask altogether?

b Which continent would you guess this park is on? Explain how you worked it out.

____

c Do you think the park is in a capital city or a small town? Explain your reasoning.

____

2 The researchers wanted to find out more about how many visitors went to the café. Look at the pie chart to see their findings.

Half of the interviewees who said 'Yes I plan to' did not actually end up going to the café. What was the total percentage of the interviewees that went to the café that day?

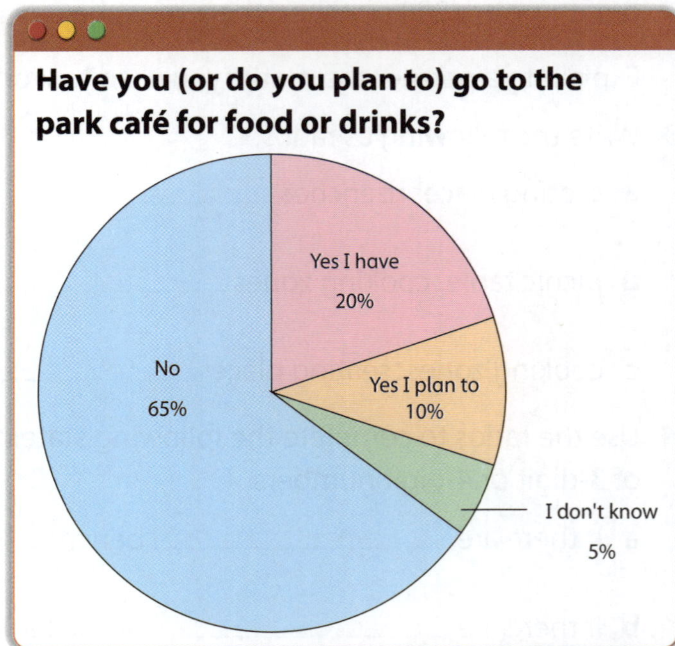

Let's solve …

3 In total, the café had 217 customers that day.
How many of them were interviewees from the survey?

Assume that the total number of interviewees who went to the café was the sum of those who said yes, and half of those who said they planned to.

4 The researchers also asked people how they found out about the park. Use the data they recorded to complete this **waffle diagram**. You can use a calculator to help you. Use a different colour or pattern for each group.

Work out the total number of answers, then work out the number in each group as a percentage of the total. If you need to, round off the percentages to the nearest 1%.

How did you find out about the park?	
Internet search	144
Someone recommended it	265
Magazine or brochure	214
Other	77

Key

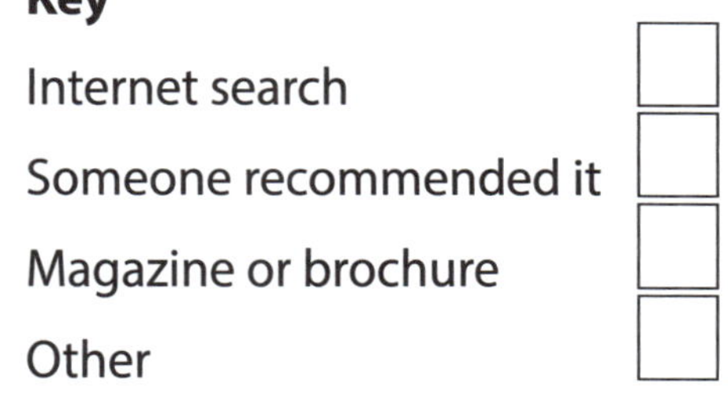

Internet search

Someone recommended it

Magazine or brochure

Other

5 Write a question of your own that the researchers could use to find out how people feel about the cleanliness of the facilities at the park. The question must be designed so that the researchers can use the answers to create a bar chart or pie chart. What would the categories be on the chart?

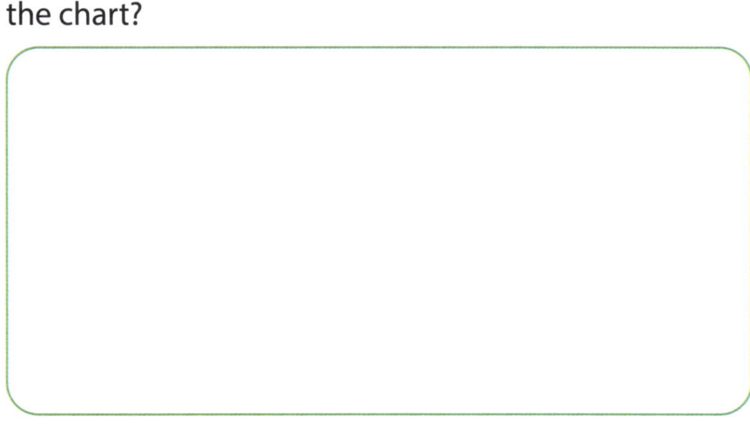

Think, talk, reason

These students are flying kites at the park. Each kite is flying at a different angle to the horizontal.

1 Estimate by looking. Whose kite is flying at an angle about double the size of someone else's? Explain to a partner how you worked it out.

____

2 Use a protractor to check. Measure the angle between the string and the base of each triangle.

a Angle ABC = _______°

b Angle PQR = _______°

c Angle JLK = _______°

Check your measurements with a partner.

3 Read what Matteo says. Explain why his reasoning works.

If you subtract angle ABC from 90 degrees, you get angle BAC. You can do the same with your other angles from question 2, to work out the angle at the top of each triangle.

Let's solve ...

The kites that people fly at the park can come in many different shapes. But in maths, a **kite** is a special type of **quadrilateral**. It must have all of these properties:

- two pairs of **adjacent** equal sides
- one pair of **opposite angles** that are equal
- diagonals that are perpendicular to each other
- the longer diagonal must bisect the shorter one (cut it into two equal line segments).

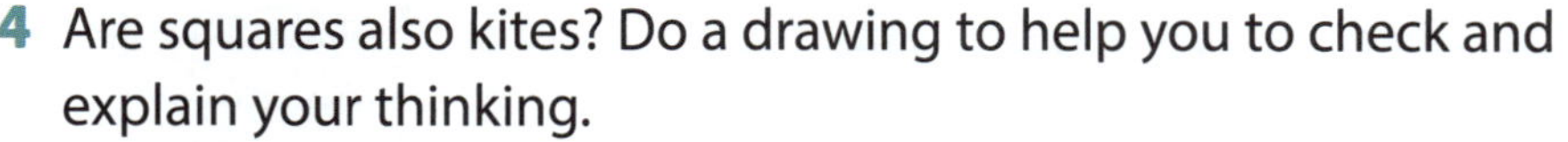

4 Are squares also kites? Do a drawing to help you to check and explain your thinking.

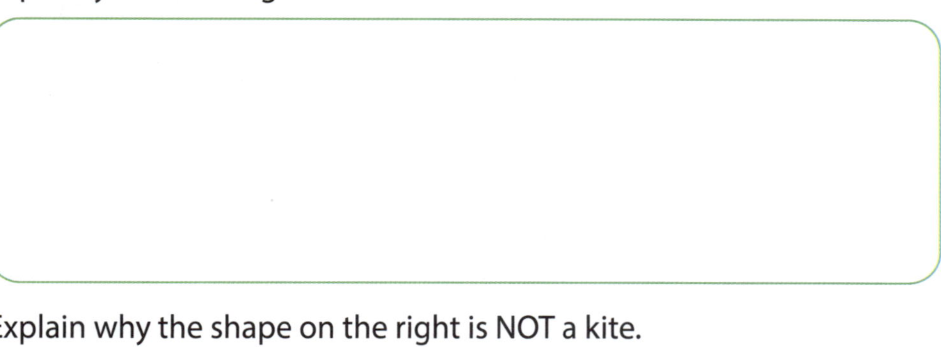

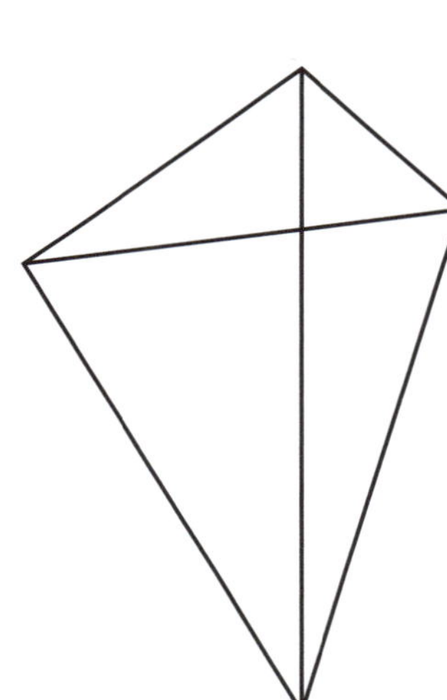

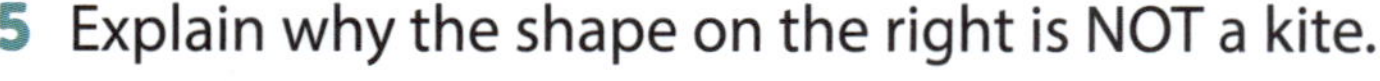

5 Explain why the shape on the right is NOT a kite.

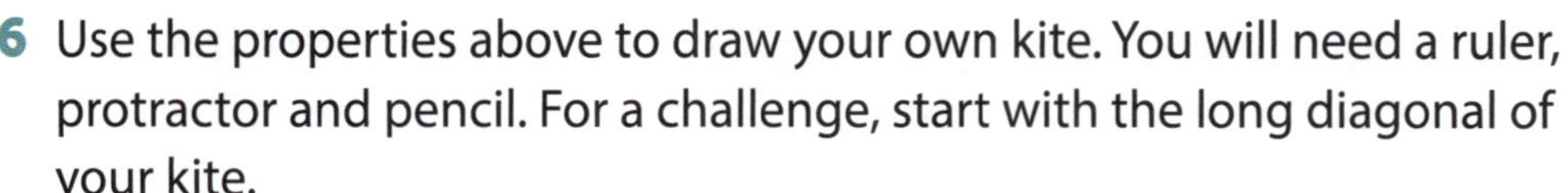

6 Use the properties above to draw your own kite. You will need a ruler, protractor and pencil. For a challenge, start with the long diagonal of your kite.

Turn back to page 4 and complete the problem-solving record.

3 Skyscrapers

Think, talk, write

1 A Stage 6 class are going to see which group can build the tallest tower. Each group may choose one or two of these materials to build with.

drinking straws

piles of paper

small blocks of wood/plastic

sweets

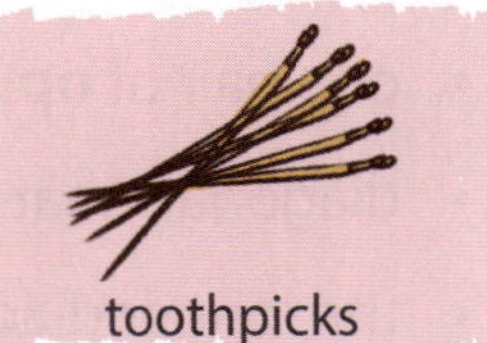
toothpicks

masking tape

toilet paper tubes

Discuss the task in your group.

- Which materials would be least suitable for making tall towers? Why?
- Which materials would you use to build the tower? Say why.
- What design would you use? Why?

2 Laila, Nomsa and Jabu all get the same task:

- **Build a tower using no more than 30 pieces of paper and tape.**
- **The completed tower must hold a 400 g tin of food for 1 minute.**
- **The tower may sag in this time, but it may not collapse.**
- **The final height of the tower is measured after that minute.**

The students sketch their final designs.

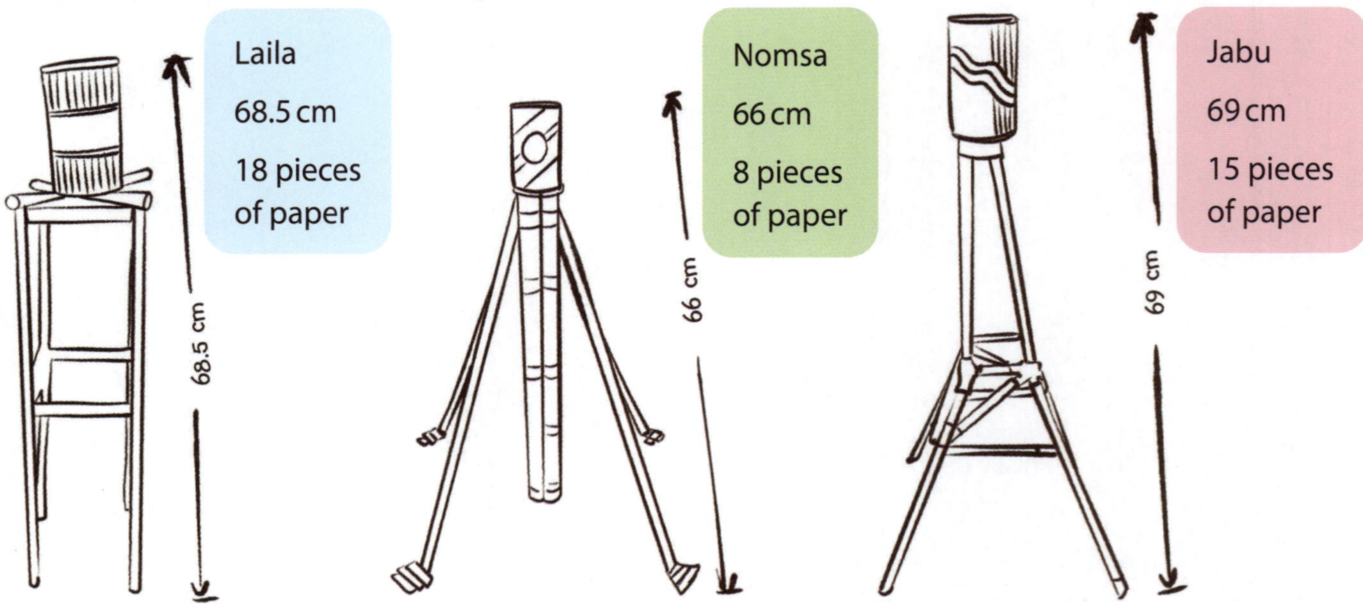

The score for a tower is worked out using this rule:

Score = (distance from the floor to the bottom of the can in cm) – (2 × the number of pieces of paper)

Work out the score for each student's tower.

Laila:

Nomsa:

Jabu:

Discuss with a partner who had the best strategy. Think about the amount of paper used and the height of the tower.

3 Sondra built a 7-storey tower using plastic cups.

Naresh says you can work out the number of cups needed for any tower like this by adding consecutively smaller numbers.

So for 8-storeys you need 8 + 7 + 6 + 5 + 4 + 3 + 2 + 1 = 36.

Sondra says there must be a rule to work this out in a faster way. She finds this rule online:

$$\frac{n \times (n + 1)}{2}$$

n is the number of storeys.

a Explain in your own words what this rule tells you to do.

b Use the rule to check the number of cups needed for an 8-storey tower.

c Work out how many cups you would need for a 12-storey tower.

Assume that they are arranged in row with each cup touching the next.

d The cups have a diameter of 7.5 cm. How wide would the base of a 15-storey tower be?

Think, talk, write

1 What does this chart tell you? What trends does it show? Share your ideas in your group.

Proportion of skyscrapers built between 2000 and 2020 in different places

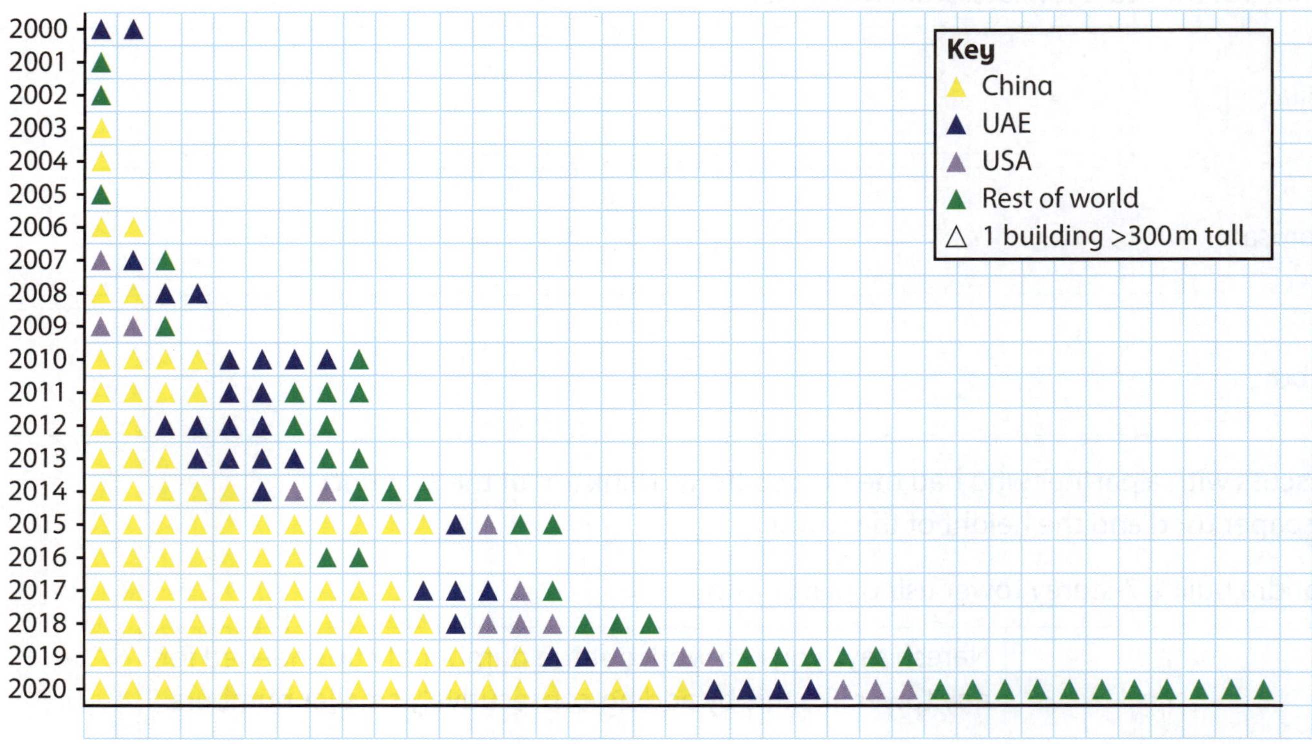

Source: Council on Tall Buildings and Urban Habitat (CTBUH)

2 Use the key from question 1 to fill in the missing information on this diagram.

Number ____________ ____________ ____________ ____________

% of total ____________ % ____________ % ____________ % ____________ %

Location ____________ ____________ ____________ ____________

Between ____________ and ____________ skyscrapers have been built. Over $\frac{1}{2}$ of these are in ____________

3 The Empire State building in New York took 410 days to build. It has 102 storeys and it is 443 m tall. The Burj Khalifa in Dubai (UAE) took 6 years to build and it is 828 m tall with 164 storeys.

At what rate was each building constructed? Work out your answer in

a metres per day: Empire State building ____________ Burj Khalifa ____________

b storeys per week: Empire State building ____________ Burj Khalifa ____________

c Burj Khalifa is almost twice as tall as the Empire State Building. Did it take twice as long to build? Suggest a reason for this.

____

4 An engineer supplied this information about how long it takes to build a skyscraper.

• Digging and constructing foundations	6 months
• Casting a concrete slab for the base	2–3 months
• Building inside structures	1 storey per week
• Finishing outside structure	2 storeys per week
• Electrics, plumbing, lifts etc.	18 months
• Testing and commissioning	6 months

a Estimate how long will it take to build a 57-storey building if each stage is completed before the next one starts

____

b The inside structure of a 60-storey building is already on storey 23. The contractors are completing the outside as they build. They are already up to storey 18. Estimate how long will it take to complete the building.

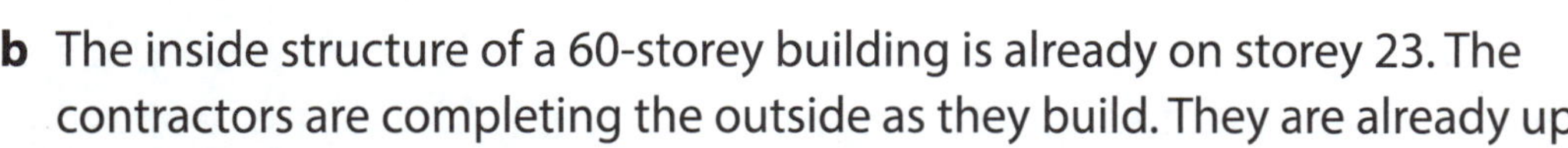

____

c In 2015, a company in China built a 57-storey building in 19 days. They could work quickly because they built parts of the building in a factory before they put them together.

How many storeys a day did the company construct? ____________

Compare this with Burj Khalifa. How much faster is it?

____

Let's solve ...

In 2023, Burj Khalifa was the tallest building in the world.

Height to tip:

- 828.8 m

Highest usable storey:

- 584.5 m (160th storey)

Outside:

- 103 000 m^2 glass
- 15 500 m^2 stainless steel

Viewing platforms:

- 555 m (148th storey)
- 452 m (124th storey)

Lifts to viewing platform:

- two double decker lifts carry 21 people per deck
- travel at 10 m per second
- start on ground floor

1 The vanity height of a building is the difference between its highest point and the highest usable storey.

a What is the vanity height of Burj Khalifa in metres?

____

b What percentage of the building's height is vanity height?

____

2 What is the average height of each usable floor in the building?

____

3 What is the difference between the amount of glass and the amount of stainless steel on the outside of the building?

____

4 Work out how much time it takes for the lifts to travel from the ground floor to:

a the 124th storey

____

b the 148th storey.

____

c If the lifts to the viewing platforms are filled to capacity and they run every half hour, how many passengers will they carry between the 9:30 a.m. lift and the 12:30 p.m. lift?

____

d When the Burj Khalifa was being built, contractors used high speed construction lifts (hoists) to move material and people up and down. These lifts travelled at a speed of 2 metres per second. Compare this mathematically with the speed of the passenger lifts.

____

5 After every 30th storey, there are two storeys for the electrical machinery and mechanical equipment. These are called mechanical floors. The first mechanical floors are on the 31st and 32nd storeys. How many mechanical floors are there between the ground and the 160th storey?

____

6 1 385 000 kg of aluminium was used in Burj Khalifa. This is equivalent to the mass of five empty A380 aircraft. The total length of the stainless steel on the building is 96 690 metres. This is 293 times the height of the Eiffel Tower in Paris.

a Calculate the mass of an A380 aircraft.

____

b How tall is the Eiffel Tower?

____

c How many Eiffel Towers high is the Burj Khalifa?

____

7 Make up a challenging two-step problem for your partner to solve using facts about Burj Khalifa.

Let's solve ...

In most buildings, people are told to use the stairs rather than the lifts in the event of a fire or other emergency. Stairwells are designed with fire-resistant materials and they provide a safer path out of the building.

1 There are 2909 stairs up to the 160th storey of Burj Khalifa. To go higher than that, there are a series of ladders.

a Approximately how many stairs is this per storey?

b What is the approximate height of each stair? Show how you work this out.

Refer to the information on page 34 to help you.

c Burj Khalifa has a special firefighters' lift that can carry 5500 kg. It has been programmed to operate during a fire. The average mass of a firefighter is 80 kilograms and they each carry 32 kilograms of equipment. How many firefighters can the lift carry?

d There are pressurized air-conditioned safety rooms approximately every 25 storeys. If you are on storey 160, the closest safety room is on storey 138. How many stairs would you need to climb down to reach it?

e If you were on storey 120, would you climb to the safety room on storey 138, or go down to the next one? Give a mathematical reason for your answer.

2 An athlete from Dubai ran up the stairs in Burj Khalifa in just over 45 minutes.

a Express this in stairs per minute.

b Do you think the athlete actually ran up that number of stairs each minute? Give a reason for your answer.

3 The longest stairway in the world is the Niesen Staircase with 11 674 stairs. It was built next to a train track in the Swiss Alps so that workers can maintain the tracks. Once a year, there is a race up the staircase. Up to 500 athletes start the race 20 seconds apart so that they can move up the narrow staircase.

The record for the men's race is 1 hour and 2 minutes and the record for the women's race is 1 hour and 9 minutes.

a 486 people take part in the race. The first athlete starts at 05:15. At what time will the last athlete start?

____

b How many stairs per minute would an athlete need to cover to beat the men's record? Show how you work this out.

c Marija trains hard and she completes the race with an average speed of 171 stairs per minute. Does she beat the women's record? Show how you decide.

Think, talk, reason

The footprint of a building is the area it covers on the ground.

1 These buildings have all been modelled at the same scale.

Discuss these questions with a partner.

a Which building will have the greatest footprint? Why?

b Which building will have the smallest footprint? Why?

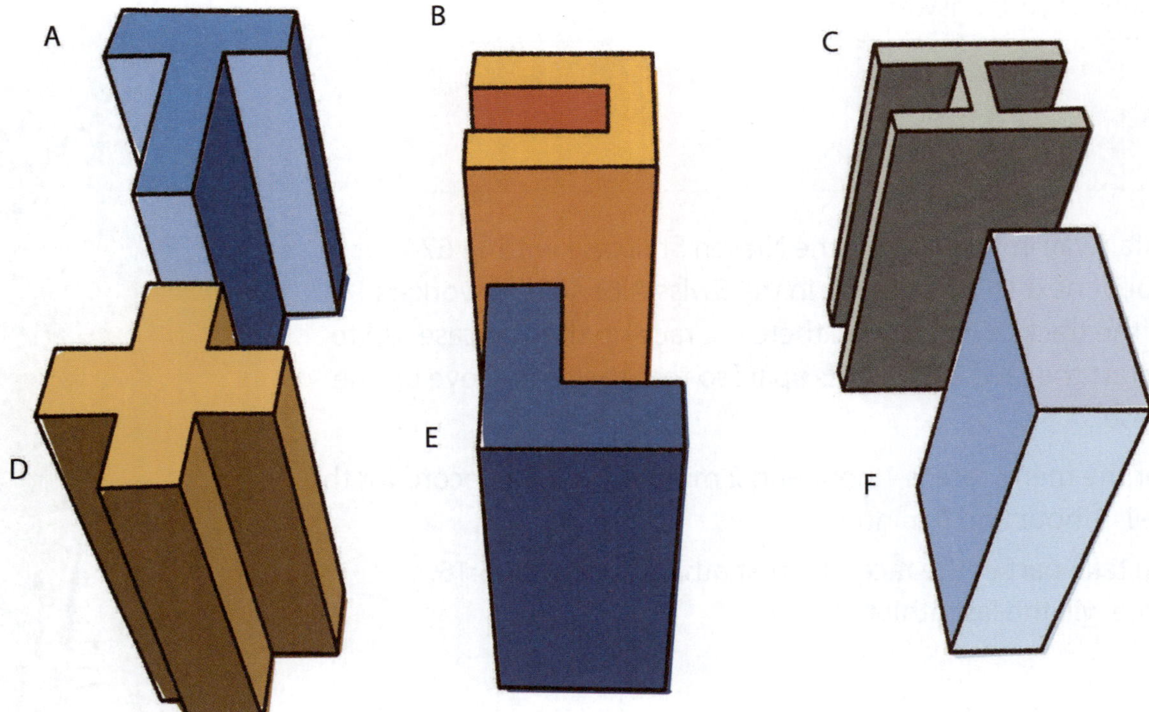

2 The buildings are all the same height. Rank them in order from greatest to smallest volume. Tell your partner how you decided.

________ ________ ________ ________ ________ ________

3 A 72-m high building has a footprint of 243 m^2. Is this enough information to work out its volume? Give a reason for your answer.

____

____

4 The shape of the footprint and height of the different sections of this building are given on the diagram.

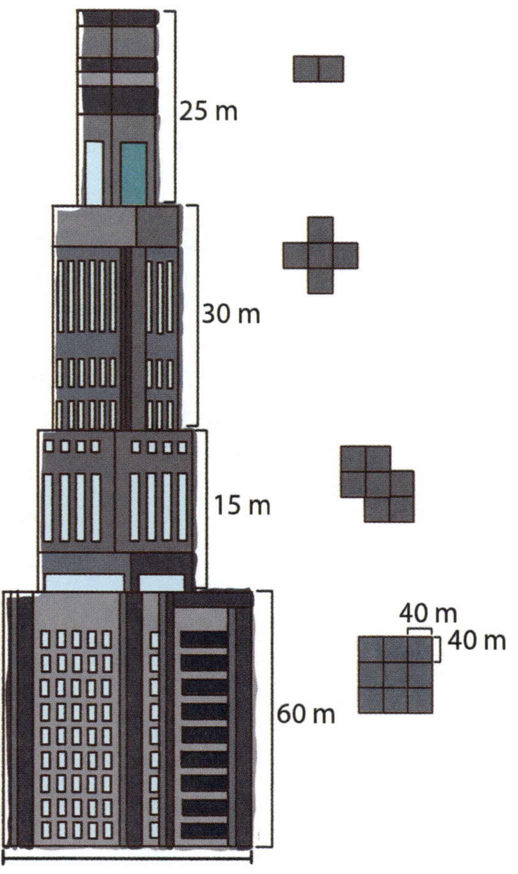

a How tall is the building?

____

b What is the area of the footprint of the lowest section?

____

c What fraction of the lowest section footprint is each of the other sections? Give your answer as a fraction and as a percentage rounded to the nearest whole percent.

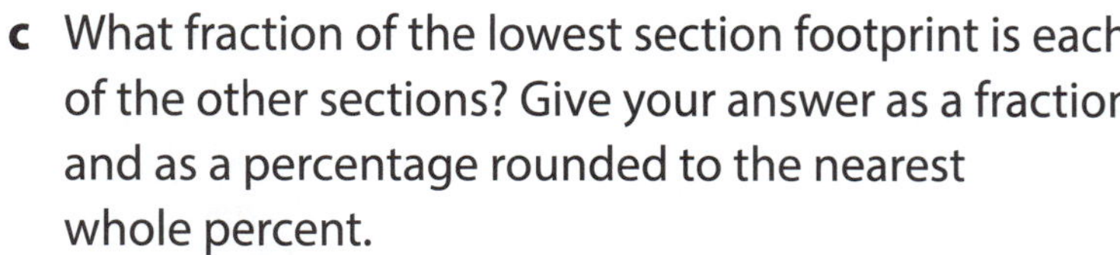

Second section: ____________ = ____________ %

Third section: ____________ = ____________ %

Top section: ____________ = ____________ %

d Calculate the volume of the whole building. Show all your calculations.

Think, talk, solve

1 Skyscraper puzzles are logic puzzles.

They consist of a square grid of $n \times n$ blocks.

The aim of the puzzle is to fill each row and column with numbers to represent skyscrapers of different heights.

The heights are from 1 to n. For a 4×4 grid, $n = 4$ and the heights are 1, 2, 3 and 4.

You may not have two skyscrapers of the same height in any row or column.

Work with a partner. Talk about this completed puzzle.

- Is it correct?
- The numbers at the side tell you how many skyscrapers you can see if you look down the row. How does this work?
- What are the two numbers you cannot see at the top of the puzzle?
- Matt says that if there is a 1 at the side, you place the tallest skyscraper next to it. Explain why.

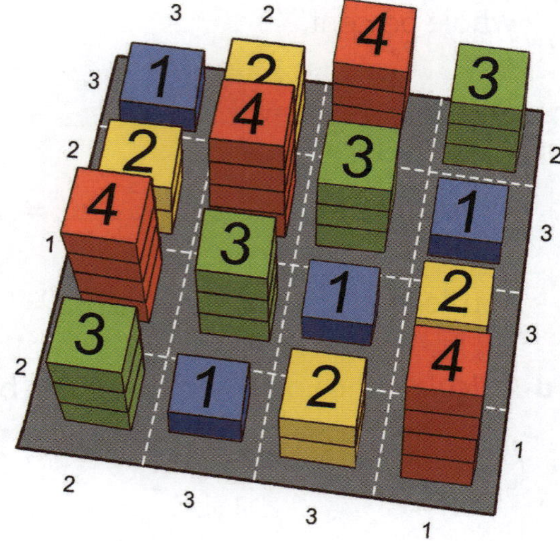

2 Try to solve this puzzle. Use different colours for each height or write numbers in the boxes.

Compare your answer with a partner. Talk about:

- What strategies did you use?
- Did you make any mistakes? What did you do about them?

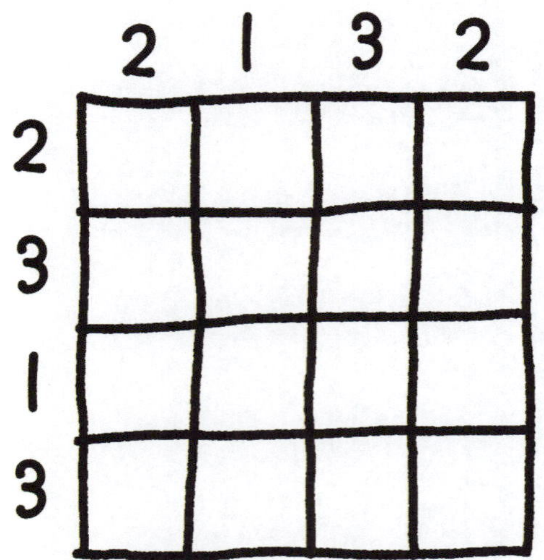

3 Here are two puzzles. Some numbers have been provided on the sides. Complete both puzzles. Fill in all the numbers in the grids and add the missing numbers to the sides. Check your solutions with your partner.

a

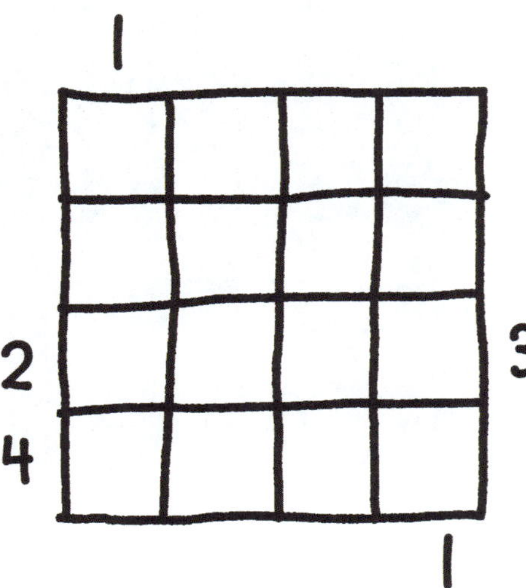

b

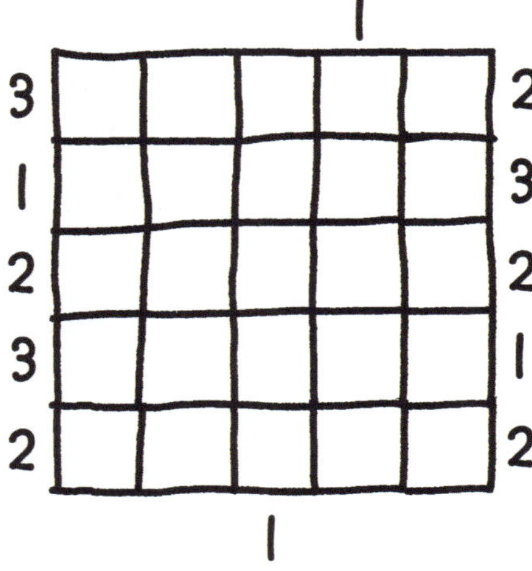

4 Look at this puzzle with a partner. What mistakes can you find here?

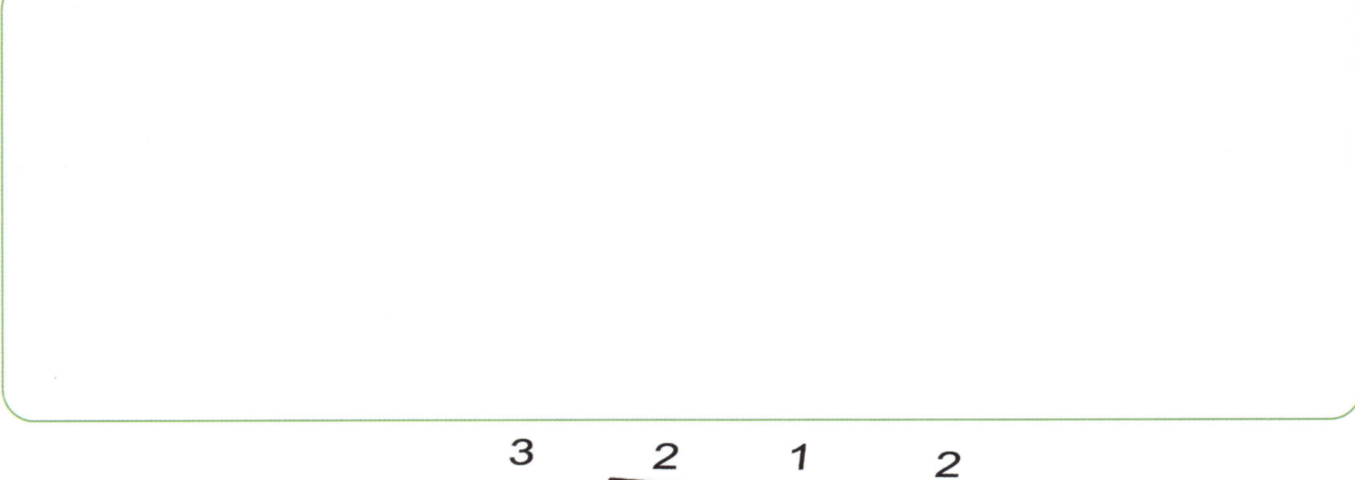

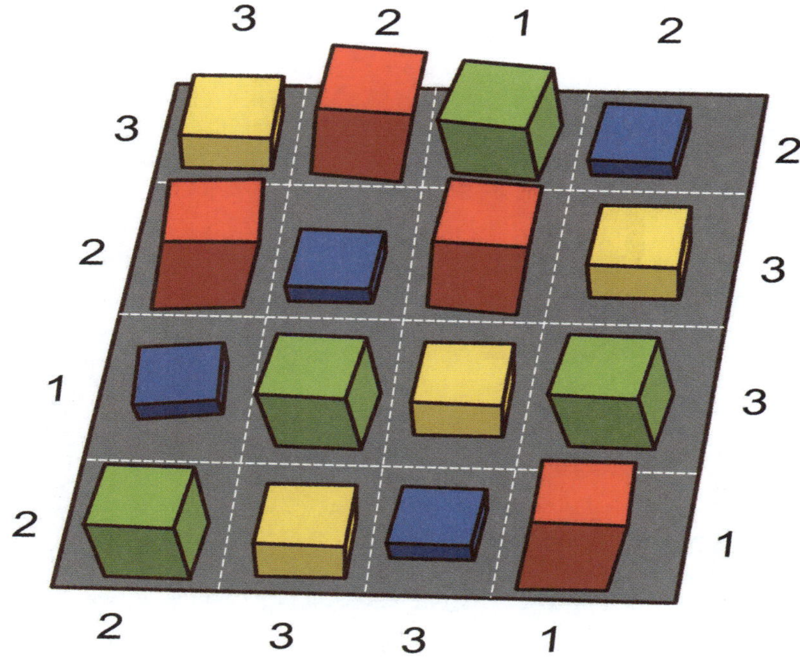

Turn back to page 4 and complete the problem-solving record.

4 Old-school games

Think, talk, reason

Some computer games have shapes that fall from the top of the screen. They have to fit into the shapes that have already landed at the bottom of the screen. The aim of the game is to have as few empty blocks as possible.

1 The grid in the picture is 20 blocks wide and 20 blocks high.

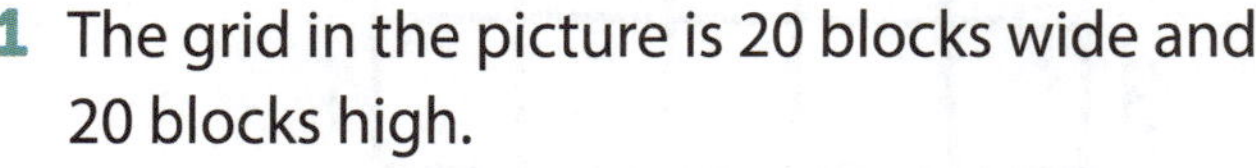

a How many blocks are there in the entire grid?

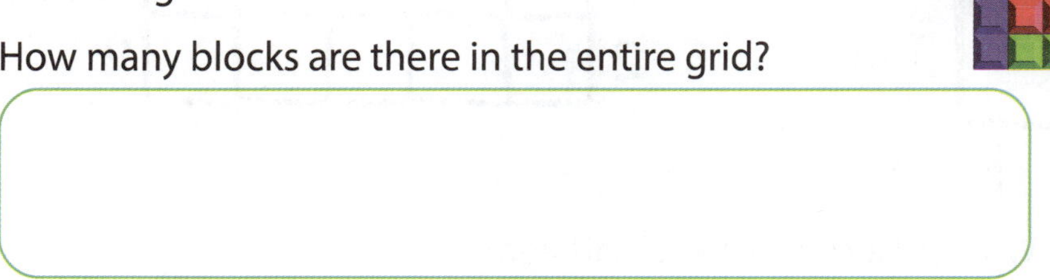

b Describe what is similar and what is different about the falling shapes.

2 A shape with two connected squares is called a **domino**.

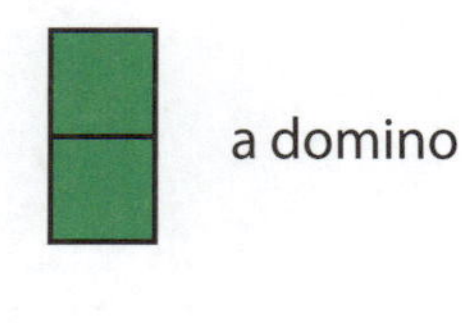

a domino

The shapes in the game are called **tetrominoes**. What do you think the prefixes 'do-' and 'tetra-' mean?

3 As the shapes fall, the player can perform different transformations on them:

rotate 90 degrees

translate horizontally left or right.

For each shape below, circle the shape that is not formed by rotating the first shape.

a

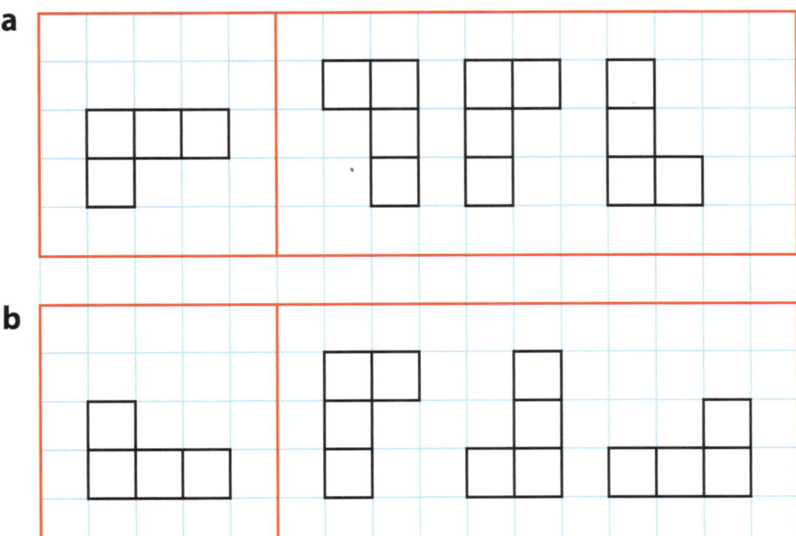

b

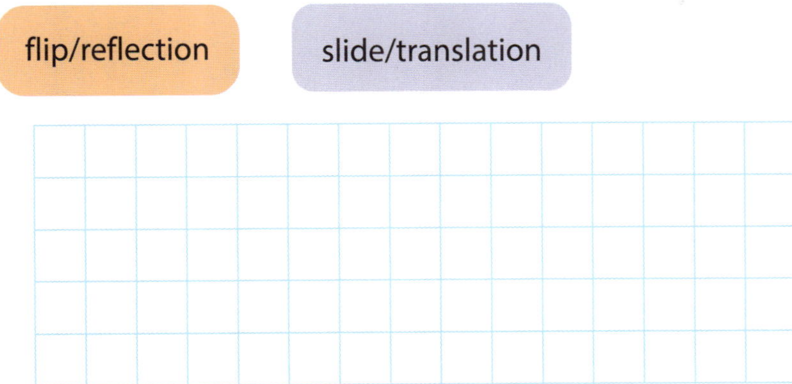

4 Which of the following terms best describes the odd shape out in part b above? Draw a diagram to explain the meaning of the term you chose.

flip/reflection

slide/translation

5 **a** Draw the reflection of this tetromino.

b Imagine that you could translate each of the four blocks one by one. Tell a partner how you could translate them to create the same result as your reflection.

You can give them letters A, B, C and D, and say how you would translate each one.

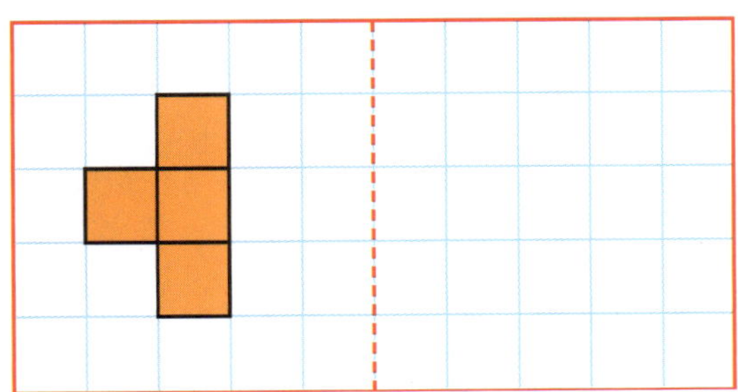

These children have been playing computer games. They used riddles to share their scores.

Read each clue carefully. Decide which part of the number you need to work out first.

1 Use your calculator to work out their scores. Make notes about your strategy in the working space – for example, what you worked out first, and what each calculation told you to do next.

If you multiply 7850 by half of 194, you get my score.

Zoe

Score

My score is a 7-digit number. The digits in the millions, thousands and ones places are all 9s. There is a zero in the ten-thousands place. The other digits are all fives.

Bruno

Score

My score is double Zoe's, plus a hundred thousand.

Mila

Score

To get my score, add 9 million to the product of 48 and 9368.

Khaled

Score

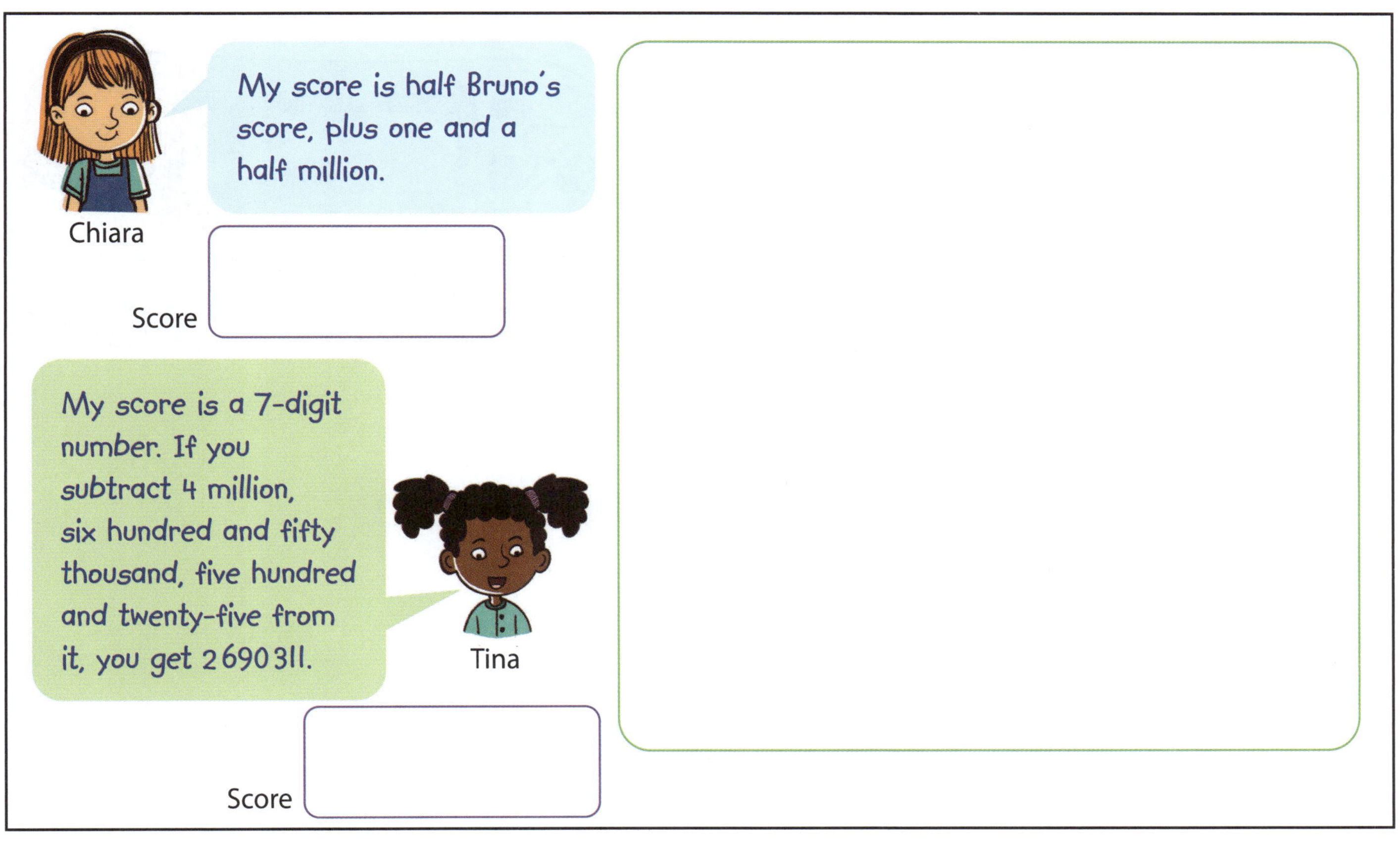

2 Choose one of the score totals. Write your own riddle for a partner to solve. Did they work out the correct answer?

Think, talk, solve

Nur's electronic game has lights in different colours and shapes above the screen.

The lights and sound effects follow this pattern:

- The round red lights flash every 3 seconds.
- The yellow triangular lights flash every 4 seconds.
- The blue square light flashes every 5 seconds.

1 Nur records information about the ways the lights flash:

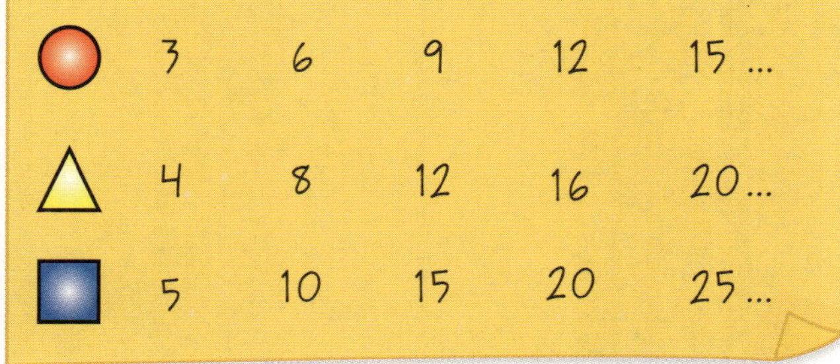

○	3	6	9	12	15 ...
△	4	8	12	16	20...
□	5	10	15	20	25...

What did Nur use the numbers to show?

____

2 Work with a partner. Use Nur's number sequences to work these out.

a After how many seconds will the ○ and the △ flash together?

____

b After how many seconds will the △ and the □ flash together?

____

c After how many seconds will all three colours flash together?

____

3 Nur plays the game for 3 minutes 20 seconds. Work out how many times each light flashes in this time.

Let's solve …

Juma and Ava play a different game. This one has lights, beepers and buzzers.

- The lights flash every 10 seconds.
- A buzzer sounds every 6 seconds.
- A beeper sounds every 15 seconds.

4 Think about the way Nur recorded information about the flashing lights. Juma and Ava started recording the information about their game in different ways.

Juma

Light	10, 20
Buzzer	6, 12
Beeper	15, 30

a Continue to fill in the table so that each row has six terms.

b What did Ava do differently to Juma?

____

c Tell a partner what each of Ava's symbols represent. Fill in the rest of the symbols in the correct places around the circle.

5 Use the work you did in question 1 to work out how many times per minute:

a the lights flash and the buzzer goes at the same time ______________________________

b the buzzer and the beeper go at the same time ______________________________

c the lights and the beeper go at the same time ______________________________

d everything happens at the same time ______________________________

6 Work out how many times each thing happens in a 5-minute game.

a lights flash ☐ **b** buzzer sounds ☐ **c** beeper sounds ☐

Think, talk, reason

In a computer game called Moonrock Leaps, the astronaut must jump over all the moon rocks on the screen before the time runs out. When the astronaut has jumped over all the moon rocks, a new screen appears, with a higher number of moon rocks.

In the first screen of Level 1, there are 5 moon rocks. In each screen after that, there are 3 more than the previous level. There are 20 screens in a level.

1 How can you work out the number of moon rocks in the 10th screen? Look at what these students did. Discuss with a partner and answer the questions that follow.

Ahmed

Screen	1	2	3	4	5	6	7	8	9	10
Rocks	5	8	11	14	17	20	23	26	29	32

The rule is start with 5, and add 3 for each new term.

Tristan

1 ⟶ $5 + (3 \times 0)$

2 ⟶ $5 + (3 \times 1)$

3 ⟶ $5 + (3 \times 2)$

4 ⟶ $5 + (3 \times 3)$

So 10 ⟶ $5 + (3 \times 9)$

This number is 1 less than the screen numbers.

a Who got it right? How do you know?

b Whose method made it easier to work out the 10th screen?

c Use Tristan's method to work out the number of rocks on the 20th screen in Level 1.

2 In Level 2, the first screen has 7 rocks, and each screen after that has 4 more than the previous screen. Work out the number of rocks on the 15th screen.

3 In Level 5, the first screen has 4 rocks. Each screen increases by 2 more than the previous one. How many rocks are there on the 7th screen?

4 Write your own problem based on another level of Moonrock Leaps.

Let's reason …

In this game, some of the grass is hiding an egg! If you click on an egg, you will break it, so you must work out where they are hiding. As you uncover blocks, you reveal one of the following:

This is a block that has no eggs and is not touching any blocks with eggs.

Oh no! You broke an egg! You lose!

This block has no eggs, but one of the **adjacent** blocks does – that is, one of the blocks with an edge or corner touching this one.

This block has an egg, and you have safely uncovered it.

You use the numbered blocks as clues to work out where the eggs are.

1 Look at the arrangements of blocks.

a When you start the game, you click a block at random. What is the greatest possible number of eggs it can show? Explain how you worked it out.

b A block has eggs on $\frac{1}{4}$ of its adjacent squares. The number it will show is ☐

c If a block has eggs on $\frac{3}{4}$ of its adjacent squares, the number it will show is ☐

d If a block shows 1, ☐ of its adjacent squares have eggs. (Write a fraction.)

2 Megan has just started a game. She uncovers this section.

a Which block/s should she mark as hiding an egg? Draw a dot on those blocks.

b Tick the block/s you think it would be safe to uncover next.

c Explain to a partner how you decided.

3 In another area of the board, she uncovers these numbers.

a Which two blocks definitely have eggs? Put dots in those blocks.

b Tick the block/s that definitely do not have eggs.

c Explain to a partner how you decided.

4 Sometimes when you click on a block, a lot of blocks get cleared at the same time. This gives you clues about what you can safely click next. In this screen, tick at least four blocks that are safe to clear. Draw dots in at least three that definitely have eggs.

5 This table shows you the different levels of the game. Calculate the missing numbers.

Level	Number of rows	Number of columns	Total number of blocks	Number of eggs	Fraction of blocks that have eggs
Beginner	9	9		10	
Intermediate	16	16		40	
Expert	16	30		99	

Think, talk, reason

This chart below shows how children's time on the internet has increased over a period of ten years.

Children's internet consumption by age

Estimated weekly hours, 2007 to 2017

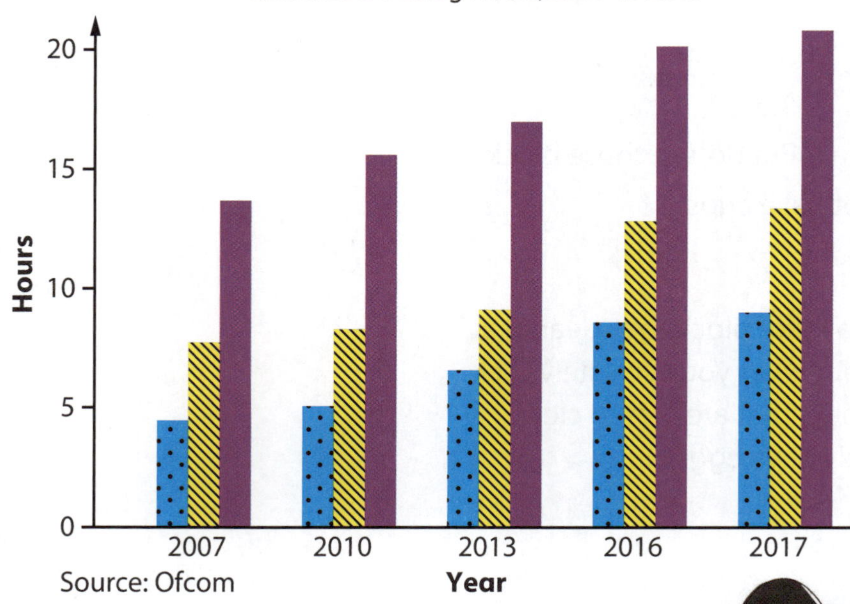

1 Julia looks quickly at the chart and says:

The data must be wrong, because it shows that, by 2016, some children were spending 20 hours per day on the internet.

What is Julia's mistake?

2 Describe the pattern you notice in the chart.

3 Instead of one bar for each year, this chart uses three. Why do you think the information is shown like this?

4 What do you notice about the dates that are represented on the chart? How could they be misleading?

How much time do students in your class spend on computers or other screen-based forms of technology?

5 Bevan decided to find out how much time his classmates spend playing on screens such as gaming devices, laptops or tablets. Bevan used this table to record the data. However, he forgot to complete the totals, and he left out Caro's data.

The mean average of a data set is the sum of the data values divided by the number of values in the set.

a Work out the totals and use these to calculate the average (mean) number of daily hours for Eline, Nadia and Issy. Round off to one decimal place.

Name	Mon	Tue	Wed	Thurs	Fri	Sat	Sun	Total	Mean
Eline	$3\frac{1}{2}$	1	0	2	2	5	7		
Nadia	4	2	0	2	4	5	7		
Issy	0	0	0	0	0	7	9		
Caro									

b Caro's total number of hours was approximately equal to 10 times one of the other students' averages. Nadia says Caro must have the highest total. Eline disagrees. Which student is correct? Why?

c The mean of Caro's hours, rounded to the nearest decimal place is 3.3. Make up a possible set of hours for Caro's week that would produce the same mean.

d Issy is only allowed gaming on the weekends. Can you think of advantages and disadvantages to this rule? Write your ideas.

Turn back to page 4 and complete the problem-solving record.

5 Caring for nature

Think, talk, solve

Protected land is any area that is legally defined and managed to **conserve** natural resources – including plants and animals that live there.

1 The table gives you data about the area of land that was protected in some countries at the start of 2022.

a Discuss the table with your partner.

- What do you notice?
- What questions can you ask?

Country	Area of protected land (km^2)
Greenland	885 647
Canada	926 034
United States of America	1 247 228
Venezuela	496 701
Peru	408 714
Brazil	2 468 479
Bolivia	336 406

b The table does not tell you what proportion of each country's total land is protected. What information would you need to work this out? Share your ideas in your group.

2 The total area of Brazil is approximately 8 515 770 km^2.

a If the empty circle represents the total area, work out what fraction of the land is protected. Show it in the circle.

b 334 352 km^2 of the protected land in Brazil is threatened by human activity. Show this clearly on the diagram. You can show your working here.

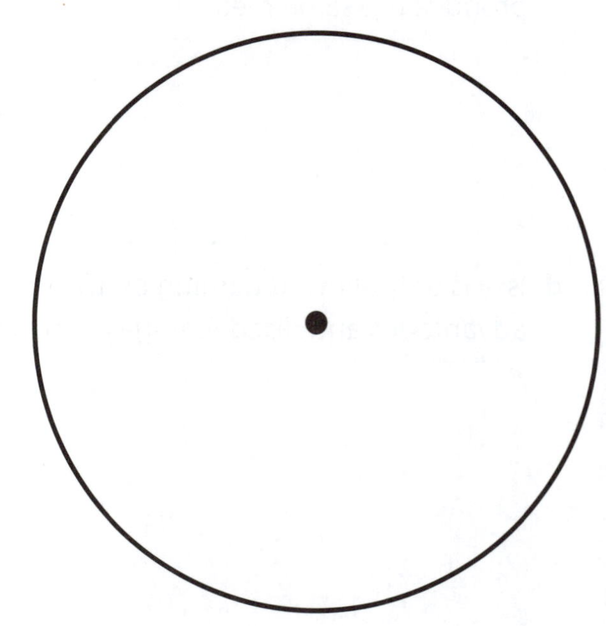

3 Juan used a computer app to draw these three diagrams. The black outer circle represents the total land for each country.

a Which country is greatest in area? ______________________

b Which country has the greatest proportion of protected land? ______________________

c Which country's protected land is most threatened by human activity? Explain how you decided.

____

____

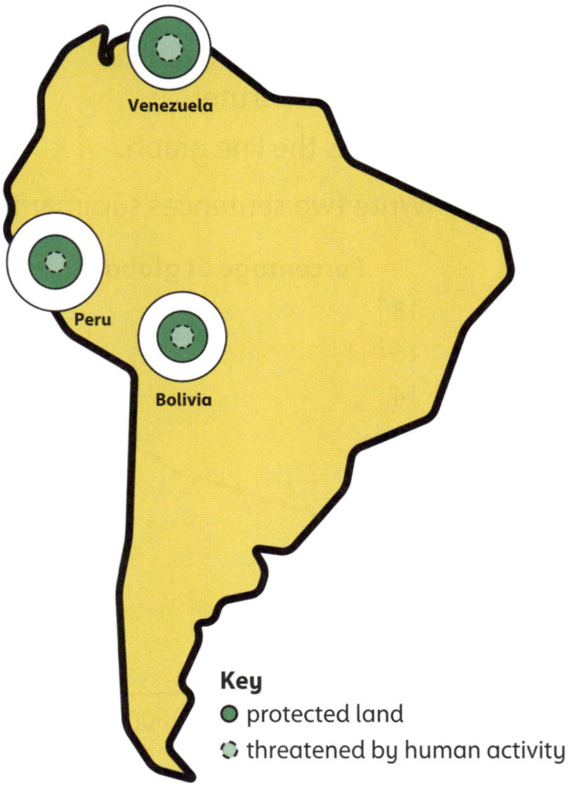

Source: Jones, K. R. et al. (2018). One-third of global protected land is under intense human pressure. *Science (New York, N.Y.)*, 360(6390), 788–791.

4 The bars show data for a country at the start of 2022. The total area protected in 2022 was 1 345 067 km^2.

Calculate the area of land that would need to be added to the protected land to meet the target for 2025.

Area conserved: 13.5%

Target for 2025: 25%

Think, talk, solve

1 Work with a partner.

- Discuss the line graph.
- Write two sentences summarizing what the graph tells you.

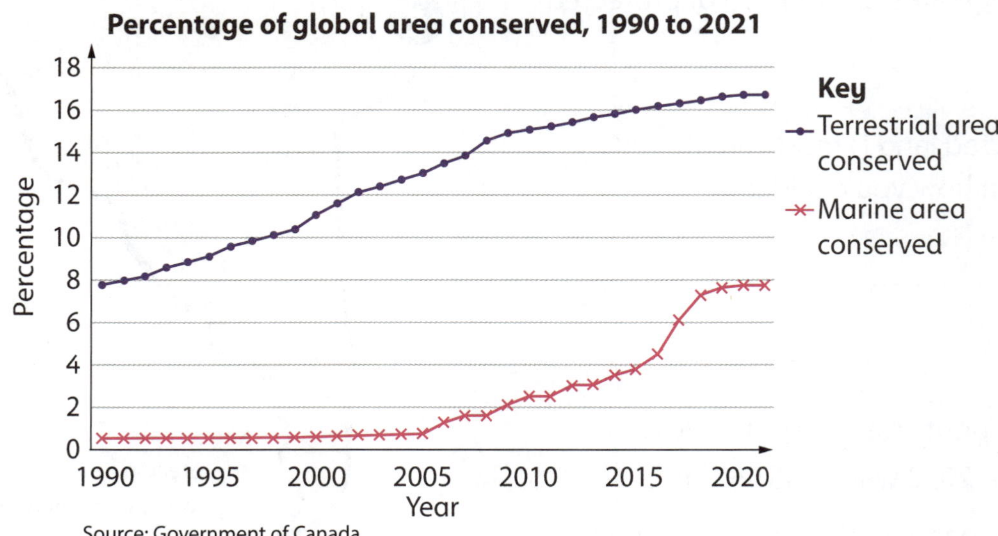

Source: Government of Canada

2 Rajesh is a journalist. He is preparing this table for a news article about reforestation in India.

	Area (km^2)		**Increase in area**	**% increase**
	2021	**2019**		
Forest cover	713 789	712 249		
Tree cover (smaller areas outside forests)	95 748	95 027		
Total				

Source: Indian State of Forest Report 2021

a Work out the missing figures and complete the table.

b Write a suitable heading for the table.

c If the total forest cover increased 1.2% by 2023, what area would be covered in forest then?

3 Jiya was interested in forest cover in large cities. She found this information.

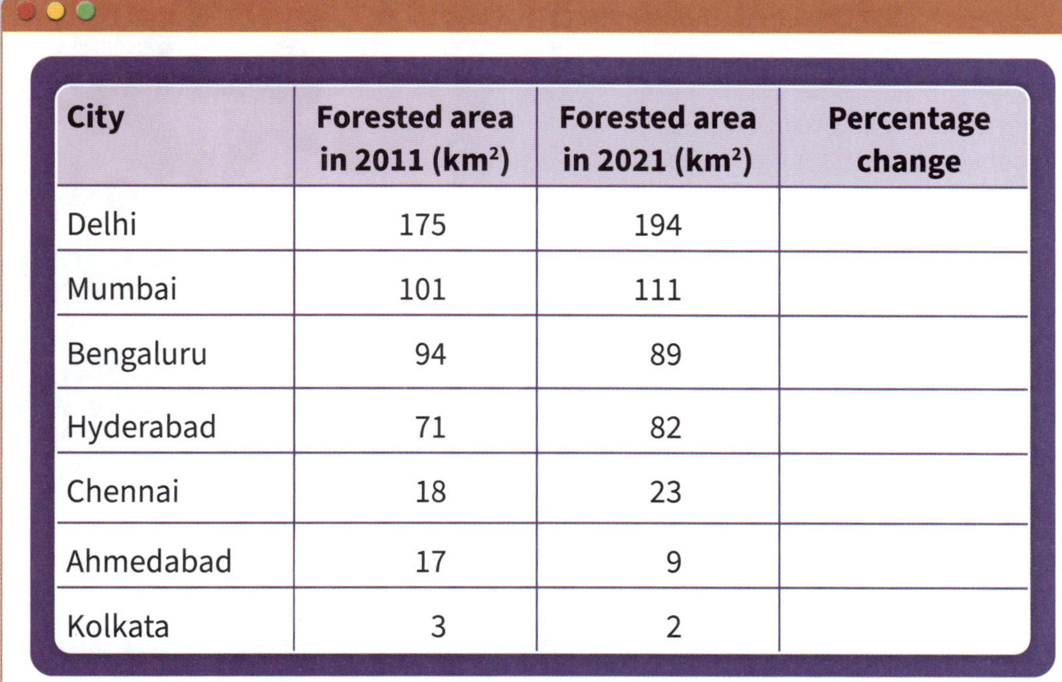

City	Forested area in 2011 (km²)	Forested area in 2021 (km²)	Percentage change
Delhi	175	194	
Mumbai	101	111	
Bengaluru	94	89	
Hyderabad	71	82	
Chennai	18	23	
Ahmedabad	17	9	
Kolkata	3	2	

Source: Indian State of Forest Report 2021

a Which city had the greatest increase in forest cover between 2011 and 2021?

____

b Which city lost almost half of its forest cover between 2011 and 2021?

____

c Calculate the percentage change for each city.

Some percentages might be negative.

4 Canada is home to 9% of the world's forests. The total area of Canada is 9 979 685 km² and, in 2022, 3 470 690 km² of the land was forest.[1]

a What percentage of Canada's land area was forested in 2022?

____

b Use the infographic to work out the total area of forest that was damaged in 2022.

____

c What is this as a percentage of the total forested area?

____

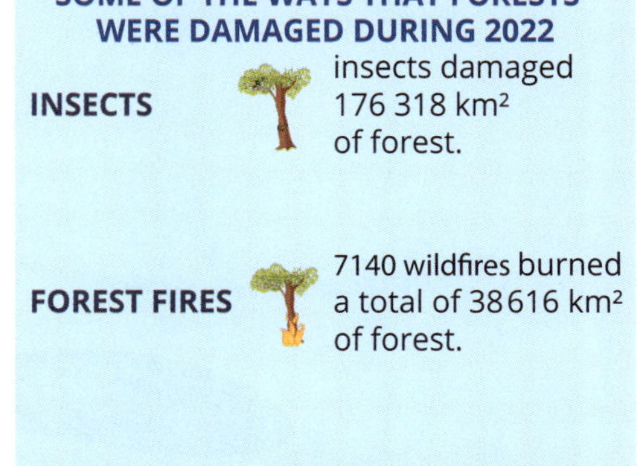

Source: Statistics Canada

[1] Source: Statistics Canada

Let's reason …

1 Tariq organizes hikes to teach students about conservation. He makes his own trail mix so that the students have a healthy snack without plastic packaging.

Tariq mixes five ingredients in these proportions:

$\frac{1}{4}$ pumpkin seeds

$\frac{1}{5}$ sunflower seeds

$\frac{1}{4}$ raisins

$\frac{1}{5}$ cranberries

$\frac{1}{10}$ chocolate chips

a Write a fraction to complete each sentence.

Pumpkin seeds and raisins together make up ________ of the trail mix.

Cranberries and sunflower seeds together make up ________ of the trail mix.

The amount of chocolate chips is ________ of the amount of cranberries.

b Complete this table to show how many grams of each ingredient there will be in 100 grams of trail mix.

Pumpkin seeds	Sunflower seeds	Raisins	Cranberries	Chocolate chips

c Tariq made 1 kilogram of trail mix and put it into 100-gram bags. Patti took one of the 100-gram bags and picked out the raisins. When she weighed them, she found that there was 20 grams of raisins in her bags. Does this mean that Tariq did not add the ingredients in the correct proportions? Discuss this with a partner.

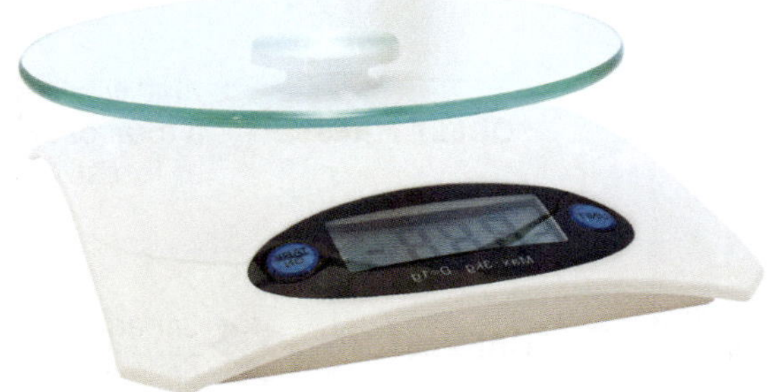

2 Tariq makes different sized bags depending on the length of the hike.

a Complete the table to show how many grams of each ingredient there would be in these packs.

Mass of pack	**250 grams**	**380 grams**	**720 grams**
Pumpkin seeds			
Sunflower seeds			
Raisins			
Cranberries			
Chocolate chips			

b What maths did you do to work out the answers? Did you find any shortcuts? Tell your partner.

3 Tariq has $3\frac{1}{2}$ kilograms of cranberries. How much of each of the other ingredients will he need to add to make his trail mix in the correct proportions? Show your working.

4 Julie does not like raisins. She changes the proportions of the mix like this:

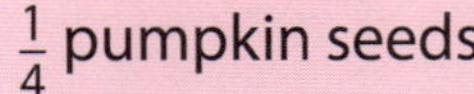

$\frac{1}{4}$ pumpkin seeds

$\frac{1}{6}$ sunflower seeds

__ mini-pretzels

$\frac{1}{6}$ cranberries

$\frac{1}{3}$ chocolate chips

What fraction of the mix will be mini-pretzels?

Think, talk, write

1 Cece and Benito visit a pond in the conservation area near their home. The first thing they see is this flock of coots.

How many birds are in this flock?

____

Tell your partner how you made sure you counted them all.

2 The average mass of a male coot is 700 grams. The average mass of a female coot is 620 grams. What is the combined mass of this flock if one-third of the birds are male?

____

____

3 Coots lay 6 to 10 eggs per **brood.** If all the female coots laid eggs, what is the **minimum** and **maximum** number of eggs you would expect?

____

____

4 About 40% of coot nests contain at least one 'parasite' egg. A parasite egg is laid in the nest by another bird. If there were 196 nests in a wildlife reserve, how many of these would you expect to have parasite eggs?

5 Cece and Benito also find purple gallinules at the pond. Gallinules are 26 to 27 cm tall. The average mass of male birds is 257 g and the average mass of female birds is 215 g. Gallinules lay 5 to 10 eggs per brood. The eggs take 19 to 22 days to hatch.

a Benito spots a male and female bird standing on a large lily leaf. Approximately what mass is the leaf supporting?

b There are 4 pairs of birds near the pond. If each pair produces the maximum number of eggs, how many eggs will there be?

c If 82% of the chicks survive, how many baby gallinules will there be?

d The eggs in one nest hatched after 20 days, on 7 April. When were they laid?

You cannot have a fraction of a bird, so give your answer to the nearest whole number.

6 Cece reads that the population of gallinules in the reserve has decreased by 3% per year over the past 15 years.

If there were 100 birds to start with, how many birds would be left after 15 years at this rate of decrease?

Explain how you worked this out.

Think, talk, reason

1 Nepal is a small country in Asia. Many tourists visit the country to hike across the Himalayas and to see tigers in their natural habitat.

Proportion of the area of Nepal that is made up of different types of protected land

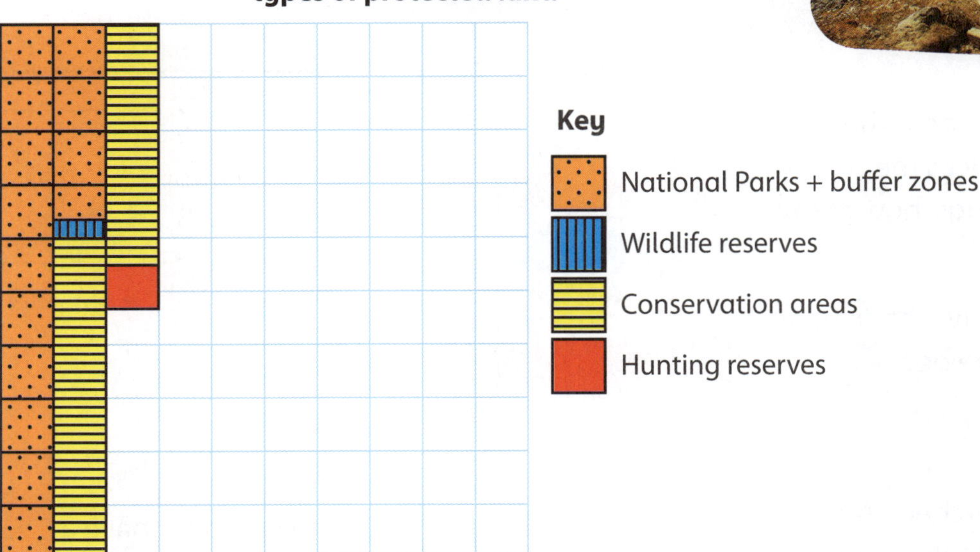

Source: Government of Nepal

Work in pairs.

a What are the different types of protected land in Nepal?

____

b All of the National Parks have a buffer zone between them and unprotected land. What do you think a buffer zone is for?

____

c Parsa Wildlife Reserve has an area of 627 km^2 and Chitwan National Park has an area of 953 km^2 and a buffer zone of 285 km^2. The two parks share a boundary. What is their combined area?

d The combined area of all the protected land in Nepal is approximately 37 237 km^2. How can you use this information to estimate the total area of Nepal? Write your ideas and solutions.[1]

[1]Source: Government of Nepal, All India Tiger Census Report

2 In 2010, Nepal had 121 tigers. It joined with governments around the world to sign an agreement that aimed to double the number of tigers by 2022.

At the end of 2022, the tiger population in Nepal was 355.

Did the Nepalese government meet its aims?
Explain your answer.

____

____

3 In a tiger census in 2018, India reported a tiger population of 2967 tigers. In 2023, the tiger census reported 3167 tigers.

a How many more tigers were there in 2023 than in 2018?

____

b Express the increase in tiger numbers from 2018 to 2023 as a percentage.

____

c Compare the number of tigers in India and Nepal mathematically.

d The International Union for Conservation of Nature (IUCN) reported that there were 5578 tigers in the wild at the end of 2022. What proportion of the world's tigers are in Nepal and India?

IUCN

Think, talk, reason

1 A conservationist says: 'Take only pictures. Leave only footprints.' In groups, discuss:

- What does this mean?
- How would following this rule help conservation efforts?

2 The summit of Mount Everest (8848.86 m) is the highest point on Earth. Each year around 800 people attempt to climb it. Local **Sherpa** guides accompany the climbers.

A group of 12 Sherpas took part in a clean-up on the mountain. They removed 1800 kilograms of rubbish.

a If each Sherpa carried an equal share of the rubbish, what mass would they each carry down?

____

b Dawa Steven Sherpa is a mountaineer. Between 2008 and 2022, he removed over 20 tonnes of rubbish from the mountain. The weather is only good enough to climb Mount Everest for 4 months of the year. Find the average amount of rubbish Dawa Steven Sherpa removed per month between 2008 and 2022.

____

c K2, in the Karakoram National Park in Pakistan has fewer climbers, but similar problems. At the end of the 2022 climbing season, nine climbers worked to remove approximately 1600 kg of rubbish on the higher slopes. Find the rate of rubbish removal using the amount of rubbish removed per climber.

____

3 The Government of Nepal plans to scan and tag all the equipment that climbers take on the mountain. The climbers will pay a $4000 **deposit**. The government repays the deposit when the climber returns with all their equipment and at least 8 kilograms of rubbish.

a What is the government trying to do? Discuss this with your partner.

b In one year, 820 climbers pay the deposit. 12% of them do not qualify for a refund. How much money will the government have to pay back?

____

____

c Do you think this is a good way to prevent littering on the mountain, or not? Share your ideas with your partner.

d Yasir Abbas, an ecologist in the Karakoram National Park says they are considering weighing climbers' equipment at the start and end of their climb. How could this encourage people to leave less rubbish on the mountain? Share your ideas with your partner.

4 In 2023, it cost £8900 for a climbing permit to go to the peak. Climbers also pay another £2000 for local companies to organize visas for their trip.

a How much money will the government receive in permit fees if 800 people apply to climb the mountain?

____

____

b The average total cost to climb Mount Everest in 2023 was £45 000. What percentage of the cost was permits and visas?

____

Turn back to page 4 and complete the problem-solving record.

6 Fast food, slow food

A group of eight friends are visiting the city of Accra in Ghana. They need to decide where to eat out. They are looking at two menus. The prices are in Ghanaian cedi (GHC).

Choose your own crust: thin, regular or thick! All prices in GHC.

Size	**Small**	**Medium**	**Large**
Diameter (inches)	12	14	18
Number of slices	8	10	12
PAPA'S FREESTYLER			
Any 2 toppings of your choice	62.00	65.00	72.00
PAPA'S CLASSIC			
Any 3 toppings of your choice	65.00	70.00	80.00

They discuss what they should do.

The Village Feast is expensive, but the portions are big, so we could share 6 dishes between 8 of us and get the discount.

If we choose the Village Feast, let's order two half-chickens, two fish and the double seafood platter. That way we can try everything.

If we get pizza, we need at least 6 slices per person.
Let's order 3 toppings on each pizza.

Our maximum budget per person is 60.00 per person per meal.

1 Look at the two menus with a partner. Discuss: If you were in this group, which menu would you find easier to choose from? Why?

2 If the students order at the Village Feast:

a What is the total before the discount?

b What is the total after the discount?

c What is the price per person?

d What percentage of their meal budget will they save with this choice? Round off to the nearest 1%.

3 If the students order at Papa's Build-Your-Own Pizza:

a How many slices do they need in total? ____________

b They would need a different number of pizzas depending on which size they choose. Complete the statement:

If we order only small pizzas, we need ____________; if we order medium, then we need ____________ and if we order large, we need ____________.

c Work out the cost per person for each option in question **b**.

____________ ____________ ____________

4 1 British pound is equal to about 14 Ghanaian cedi. Choose three of the dishes from the menu and write their prices in pounds.

____________ ____________ ____________

Think, talk, reason

Takeaway foods come in many different containers. These are all made from paper or cardboard folded into different shapes.

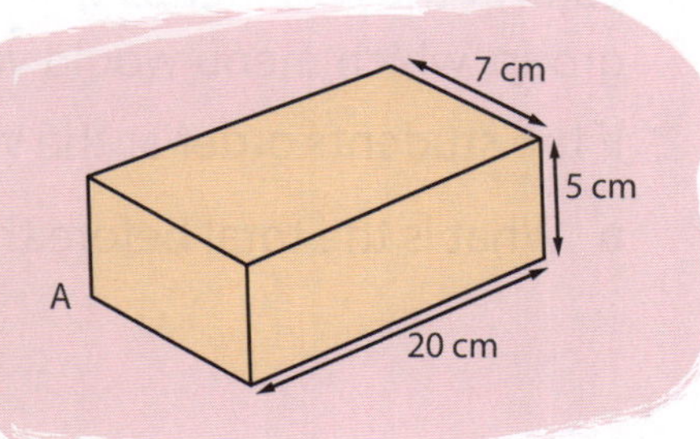

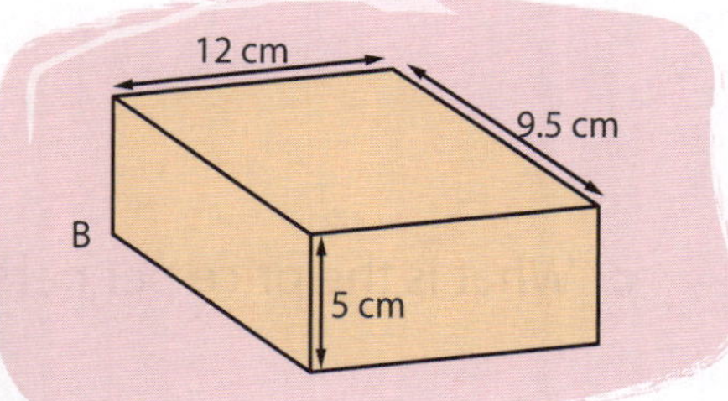

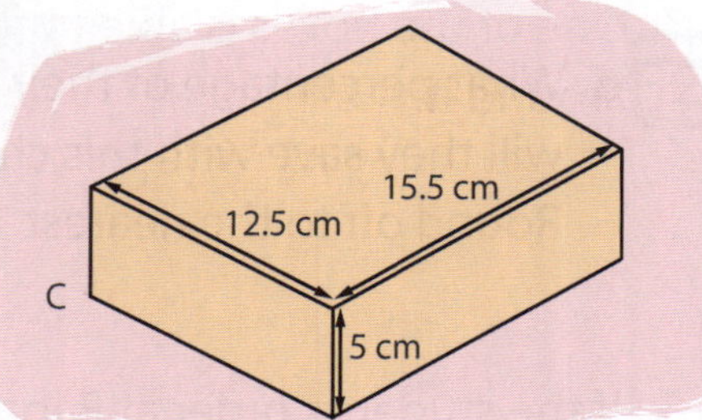

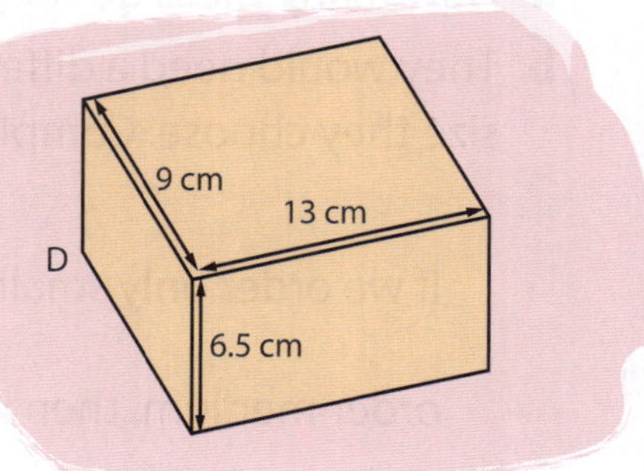

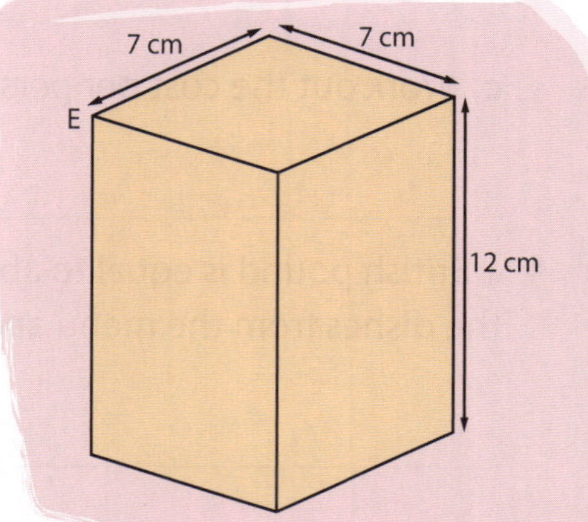

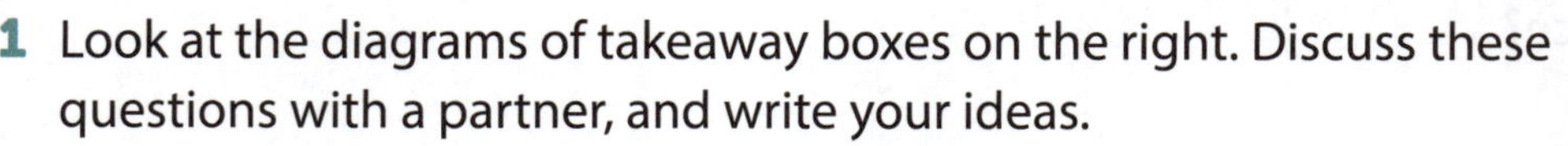

1 Look at the diagrams of takeaway boxes on the right. Discuss these questions with a partner, and write your ideas.

a How do you know that none of the shapes are cubes?

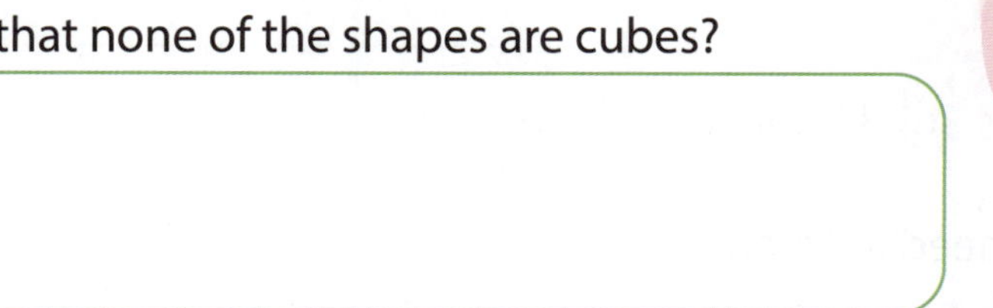

b What do they all have in common?

c Without doing any calculations, which of the boxes do you expect would have the greatest volume? Discuss your reasoning and write some of your ideas here.

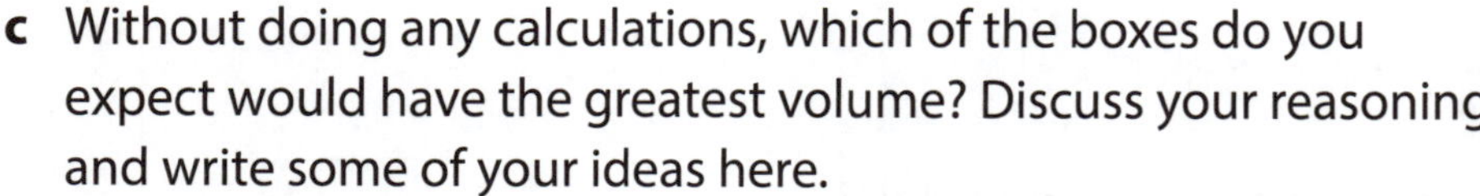

Let's solve...

Remember:
volume of cuboid = length × width × height

2 Work out the volume of each container in cm^3.

Container	Height (cm)	Width (cm)	Depth (cm)	Volume (cm^3)
A				
B				
C				
D				
E				

3 One of the boxes is able to fit inside one of the others with space around it.

a Which one is it? Explain how you checked that it could fit inside the others.

b Work out how much space is left over inside the bigger box if the smaller one is packed inside.

Think, talk solve

- 1 cup unpopped popcorn kernels = 250 g
- $\frac{1}{4}$ cup unpopped popcorn kernels makes approximately 7 cups of popped popcorn
- The average mass of one kernel of popcorn is 0.125 g
- At the supermarket, a 2 kg bag of unpopped popcorn kernels costs £3.70.
- A cinema charges £4.90 for their regular-sized box (150 g popped corn).
- The same cinema charges £5.40 for their large box (200 g popped corn).
- 1 cup of popped popcorn has a mass of about 10 g.

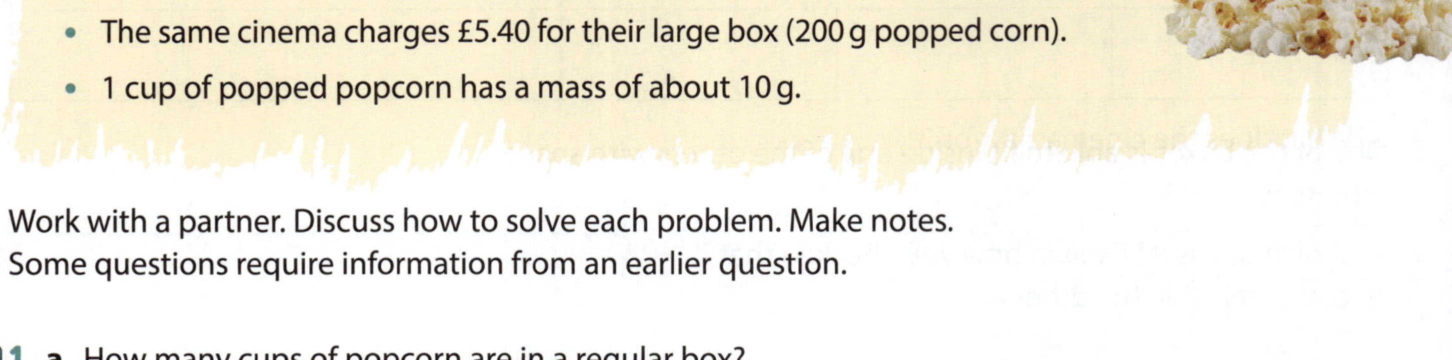

Work with a partner. Discuss how to solve each problem. Make notes.
Some questions require information from an earlier question.

1 **a** How many cups of popcorn are in a regular box? ______________________

b How many cups of popcorn are in a large box? ______________________

c What is the price per cup if you buy:

Regular ______________________ Large ______________________

2 About how many kernels are in a 2 kg bag?

3 **a** How many cups of popped popcorn can you make from a 2 kg supermarket bag of upopped popcorn kernels?

b What is the price per cup?

____

4 The cinema buys their popcorn at a price that is 30% cheaper than the supermarket price.

a What does the cinema pay for 2 kg of unpopped kernels?

____

b How much more do you pay for each cup of popcorn in the cinema than at home?

5 A popcorn machine pops 25 cups of popcorn in 5 minutes. How long will it take to pop 5 kg of popcorn?

6 Write your own word problem based on the facts about popcorn.

____

____

Think, talk, reason

Carlo and Teo are friends who live in different cities. They both have jobs delivering takeaways. Read about the deliveries the two drivers made in one night.

In my city, the restaurants are close to the areas where people live. So I make many short trips on my motorcycle. Usually, I do about 7 to 10 trips of about 3 to 5 km in a shift.

I live in a bigger city. I make longer drives with my car, so I need to make sure I collect a few orders that are all going to a similar area. Usually, I do three trips in a shift, and each trip is between $3\frac{1}{2}$ and 9 miles.

1 Discuss with a partner what calculations you would need to do to work out which driver travels the greater distance. Write your ideas here.

2 What is the shortest and longest distance that Carlo drives in a shift?

3 1 mile is approximately 1.6 km. Work out the shortest and longest distance that Teo might drive in a shift. Give your answers in km.

4 Here is a list of the distances Carlo and Teo actually drove in their shifts on the same evening.

Carlo:	**4.8 km**	**3.7 km**	**4.2 km**	**5 km**	**4.7 km**	**4.5 km**
Teo:	**7 miles**	**6.8 miles**	**8.8 miles**			

Who drove the greater average distance that night?

Let's solve...

5 A takeaway restaurant pays its drivers £12 per hour plus £2 per delivery.

If n = the number of hours a driver works, and d = the number of deliveries they make, which of these formulae would correctly work out their pay?

$(12 + n) \times (5 + d)$	$12n - 2d$
$2d + 12n$	$12n + 2d$

Explain your reasoning to a partner.

6 Work out how much each of these drivers earned for their shift.

Lucille

Quinn

Paul

7 Sometimes customers may tip the driver a percentage of the bill total. Lucille kept a note of her bill totals and the tips she received.

a Work out how much she earned altogether in tips.

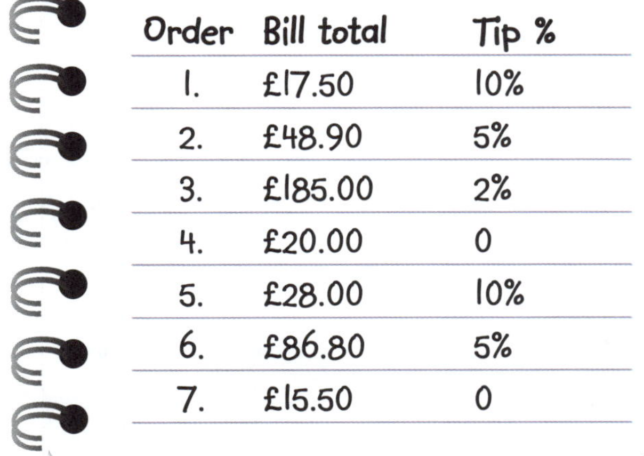

Order	Bill total	Tip %
1.	£17.50	10%
2.	£48.90	5%
3.	£185.00	2%
4.	£20.00	0
5.	£28.00	10%
6.	£86.80	5%
7.	£15.50	0

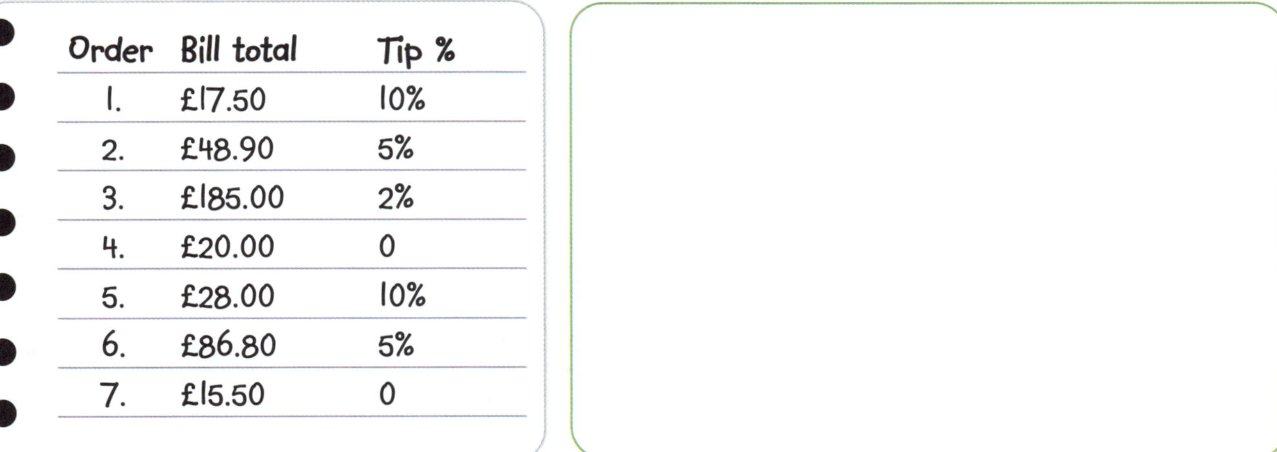

b Discuss with a partner whether there is any pattern to the way people tip. Is tipping usual in your culture? Do you think it is a fair practice? Why or why not?

Melati has a takeaway stall in Langkawi, Malaysia. She offers three types of dumplings each day. She gives the prices per plate in Malaysian ringgit (RM).

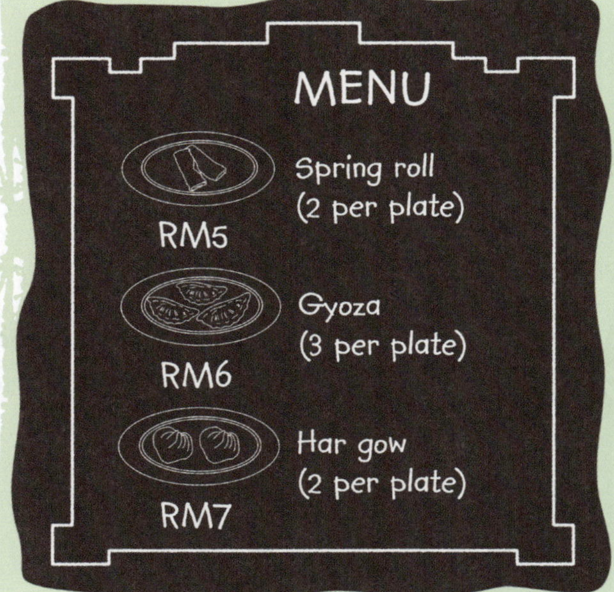

1 In a morning, Melati sells 146 plates of gyoza, 125 plates of har gow and 95 plates of spring rolls. 30% of her takings go to paying for the cost of the ingredients, fuel and cooking equipment. Her **profit** is the amount of money she makes after subtracting these costs from her income.

How much profit does Melati make that morning?

2 Discuss with a partner how you can work out the amount of profit Melati makes:

a for each individual gyoza

b for each individual spring roll.

Write your ideas.

Remember how many there are on each plate.

3 Karen and Mike are visiting Malaysia from the UK. They work out that 5 plates of gyoza cost them £5.40.

a How much does one plate of gyoza cost in pounds?

____

b How much is one ringgit worth in pounds at the time of Karen and Mike's visit?

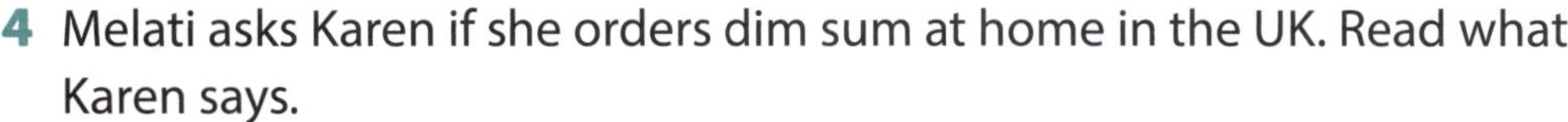

4 Melati asks Karen if she orders dim sum at home in the UK. Read what Karen says.

a How much does a plate of gyoza cost Karen in pounds when she is in the UK?

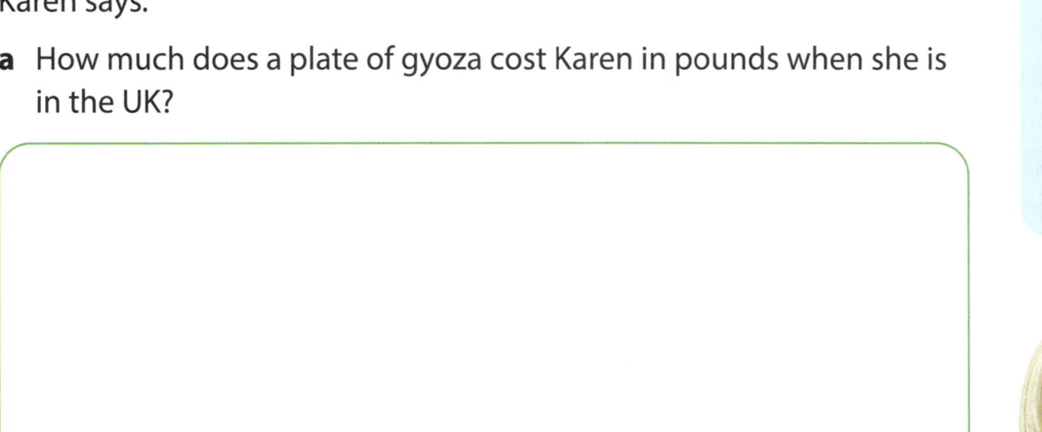

b Discuss with a partner. Why do you think prices differ so much between different countries? Where you live, is takeaway food is cheaper, more expensive or the same price as food from the grocery store? Why do you think this is?

5 A customer makes a big order for a party. She orders equal numbers of plates of gyoza and har gow. The total amount comes to RM364.

Discuss with a partner how you can work out how many plates the customer ordered of each dish. Try out your working. Check your answers – do they come to the same total?

Think, talk, reason

1 Jamila has a loyalty card from a stall where she likes to buy **lassi**, a popular yogurt drink.

a A lassi costs 60 rupees. Jamila says that when she's filled a card and had a free lassi, that is the same as paying 53.33 rupees for each lassi. How did she work that out?

b Jamila says this is an 8% discount, but she is mistaken. Jenny says it's more than 8%, and Lin says it is less than that. Who is correct? Explain your reasoning mathematically.

2 The lassi store increases their lassi price to 85 rupees. Jamila says the discount is still the same. Jenny says that's only true if Jamila starts a new card from the time the price changes. Explain mathematically what Jenny means, and whether or not you agree.

3 Jasmine has this loyalty card from an ice cream shop.

a Jasmine says the loyalty programme is the same as buy 5 get 1 free'. What is Jasmine's mistake?

---

b Each ice cream costs £1.20 for the first scoop, and 85p for each extra scoop. Jasmine always gets two scoops. How much does Jasmine still have to spend to qualify for the half-price ice-cream?

4 A takeaway restaurant has a different loyalty system. Customers earn points for each item they buy.

When you have earned 1500 points, you get £5 off your next meal.

a What is the owner doing to encourage people to buy the special?

b Patrick says that this system is unfair. Discuss with a partner and decide what you think Patrick means.

Look at how much you would have to spend to earn the discount.

c Suggest your own ideas for what might make the system fairer. Why might it be a good idea to try make it fairer?

Turn back to page 4 and complete the problem-solving record.

Glossary

General terms

botanist a scientist who studies plants

brood a group of baby birds that were all born from the same set of eggs

conserve to save from destruction or harm; to keep safe for future generations

deposit a lump sum of money, often given at the beginning of a process before further money is added

domino a shape constructed using two squares

findings the result of some research, often presented as a graph or table

investor someone who puts money into a business to help it grow. They will later earn back more money if the business performs well.

lassi a drink made from yoghurt, popular in southern Asia

maximum the highest amount possible

minimum the lowest amount possible

profit in business, this is the amount of money left after all costs have been subtracted from the total amount of money taken. For example, if a baker sells 30 cakes at $2 each, the baker has taken $60. But if the ingredients for each cake cost $1.50, the baker only makes $.50 profit per cake and so $15 profit in total.

protected land geographical areas that are set aside and managed or given protection by law (nature reserves and national parks are examples of protected land)

Sherpa a person from Tibet who acts as a guide for climbers in the Himalayan mountains. Sherpas know the Himalayan region well so ensure climbers stay safe in the mountains.

tetromino a shape constructed using four squares

Mathematics terms

adjacent next to. In a 2D shape, adjacent sides are sides which are next to each other and meet at a vertex.

kite a quadrilateral with two pairs of equal adjacent sides

opposite angle when two straight lines cross and form four angles, the angles that face each other are opposite angles; opposite angles are always equal

quadrilateral any 2D shape with four straight sides, for example, a rectangle, a rhombus, a kite and a trapezium

ratio a comparison or two or more values relating to a similar topic. For example, in a school hall, the ratio of tables to chairs is 1: 6 – for every 1 table, there are 6 chairs.

waffle diagram a diagram made up of a grid of squares (resembling a waffle) that is used to show proportion, for example, a group of 20 children are asked to select their favourite fruit. A waffle diagram of a 4 × 5 grid represents the 'whole' (20) and then the squares are coloured in using different colours to represent the number of votes each fruit gets. The finished waffle diagram is a good visual representation of the proportion of votes that each fruit gets. Waffle diagrams are often made up of a 10 × 10 grid to show percentages.

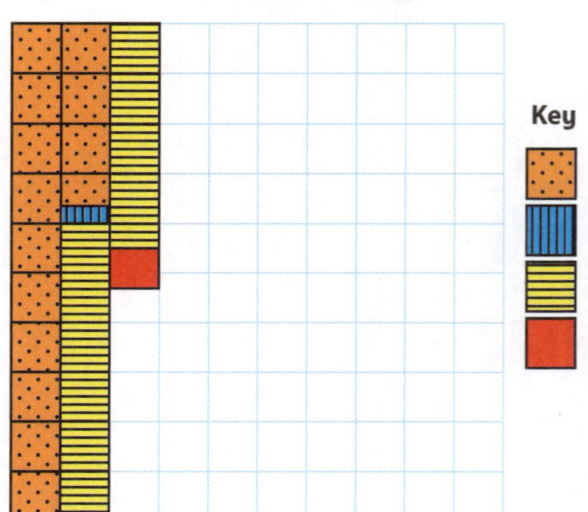